D1552292

22
Ready-Made
Prayer Services

with **100** Extra Prayer Ideas

Maryann M. Hakowski

Saint Mary's Press®

Dedication

In loving memory of Cecylia Fortuna Hakowski

May the angels bear you up;
give you to drink this holy cup.
May the Saints come welcome you;
Here is a life forever new.

(© Gary Hardin and James Hansen, "Farewell Blessing")

 Genuine recycled paper with 10% post-consumer waste. 5114100

The publishing team included Robert C. Rabe and Lorraine Kilmartin, development editors; Mary Koehler, permissions editor; interior images © 2005 www.FaithClipart .com; prepress and manufacturing coordinated by the prepublication and production services departments of Saint Mary's Press.

Jayne Stokke, cover image

Printed in the United States of America

Printing: 9 8 7 6 5 4 3 2 1

Year: 2014 13 12 11 10 09 08 07 06

ISBN-13: 978-0-88489-927-3
ISBN-10: 0-88489-927-6

Contents

Introduction

Making Room for God and Prayer

Teens today are very busy. They juggle school, jobs, sports, friends, extracurricular activities, and family responsibilities. Sometimes they see coming to church and being involved in youth activities as additional burdens.

Some say: "I give 45 minutes to God every week when I come to Mass. Isn't that enough?" And some don't even come to Mass. I encourage teens to find room for God in all they do, to find opportunities for prayer anytime and anyplace.

When I teach a Confirmation class on prayer, I always use the sponge and water illustration. I place a large empty glass on a table in front of the teens and ask, "What things in life keep you busy—fill up your life?" As they list things like work, homework, sports, and fun activities, I ask them to place a small piece of sponge in the glass. In no time, the glass is completely filled with sponges.

The teens easily agree the glass is full and their lives are even more full. I then invite a teen to pour some water into the glass. Though full of sponges, the glass holds quite a bit of water.

What happened? The water filled the spaces in and around all the sponges. Not only that, it transformed the sponges from flat and dry to soft and full.

There is always room for God and prayer in our lives, in our school, in our work, in our time with friends. Just as the sponges are changed by the water, pouring prayer into our lives will transform us as well.

Teens sometimes think prayer changes God. We can teach them that prayer actually changes the one who prays to God.

Be a Weaver of Prayer

A good storyteller is a weaver; an experienced pray-er is a weaver. You can start where you are. Look for opportunities to weave prayer into your personal life. Then, as you plan your classes or youth-group program, look for opportunities to weave prayer into all you do with youth.

You don't want to treat prayer like a Post-it note. Some people plan their whole program, realize they forgot prayer, and then try to stick it in a few places. Prayer cannot be an afterthought in a well-balanced youth ministry program. There is room for prayer in religious education classes, youth-group meetings, outreach projects, and social events. For some events, prayer is the centerpiece, such as retreats or days of recollection.

Widen Your View of Prayer

It is a good idea to begin where your young people are in their spiritual journey. Help them name the forms of prayer they already experience, such as traditional prayer (the Lord's Prayer, the stations of the cross, and so on) or prayers of petition (found in the Prayers of the Faithful at Mass.)

When teaching about symbols and prayer, consider starting with prayer symbols the young people recognize, such as a crucifix or a candle, and then challenging them to see other symbols that can invite them to prayer, such as M&M's to represent diversity, or car keys to symbolize responsibility.

There are many different forms of prayer and different ways to encounter God, but it is important to choose a prayer form that reverences the group's comfort level. For example, if your group has never experienced spontaneous shared prayer, you would be wise not to try this form the first time the group meets. You might try it later, as the teens become more comfortable with you and with one another.

Identify the gifts the teens might bring to prayer. Perhaps one plays the flute and would be willing to play a piece for meditation. Another might be a talented artist and could design the cover of your prayer or worship aid. Yet another may be good at choosing contemporary songs that add to your prayer theme for the week.

Prayer is certainly found in a Catholic prayer book or at Sunday liturgy, but it can also be found in a sunset on the beach, in a set of keys, in a song on a favorite CD, or in a grandmother's story.

We must respect how each person prays. Some find great comfort in praying the rosary in a silent chapel. Others may feel more comfortable praying by singing at the top of their lungs at a Christian rock concert. God does not care *how* we pray but rather *that* we pray. Limiting prayer to one form limits how God can touch us.

How to Use This Book

This prayer resource book has been designed with twenty-two ready-to-use prayer services on a variety of themes. Choose prayer themes that speak to the everyday issues and experiences of teens as well as themes that challenge the teens to grow, especially in the area of social-justice issues. On the opening page of each chapter, you will find a list of themes and prayer forms that each prayer service uses.

The opening page of each chapter also contains a list of extra prayer ideas. You can use these ideas as a springboard in planning lead-in or follow-up activities, in leading additional activities on related topics, or in place of the full prayer service presented in the chapter.

On the second page of each chapter is a list of materials needed, what to prepare before the prayer service, and the order of prayer to guide you in leading the prayer service. Many of the prayer services incorporate song. Unless otherwise indicated, the teens are to sing the suggested songs. You can find most of the songs in popular hymnals or worship resources. A search of the Web sites of liturgical music publishers such as OCP Publications and GIA Publications, Inc., can help you locate CDs, sheet music, and lyrics. Most of the song lyrics can also be found on the Christian Lyrics Online Web site. It is up to you to determine what will work best for your group of teens. Most of the prayer services also incorporate readings, providing the opportunity for teens to serve as lectors and prayer readers. Parts for individual readers or for the group as a whole are printed as handouts or resources at the end of each chapter. You can photocopy those and distribute them to your readers.

If you are new to youth ministry or are short on planning time, you will probably want to use the prayer services exactly as written. If you are an experienced youth minister or have ample planning time, you might want to choose individual parts of the prayer services and put them together into your own prayer experience.

Plan Ahead

Prayer can be so much more than starting your meeting with the Lord's Prayer. Plan ahead to make the experiences more meaningful. Check the teaching manual for your class, this book, and other prayer resource books to add prayers on a variety of personal, liturgical, and real-life themes.

Prepare your environment to make it appropriate for prayer. If you need quiet, choose a place more removed. If the teens need a place to spread out, choose a larger space for prayer.

Make sure those assisting with prayer understand their roles and have time to practice their readings. Check the sound system and other electronic devices you will be using to make sure they are working properly before you begin prayer.

Be Open to the Spirit

Despite all your planning, events will happen in the lives of the teens and the world around us. When someone or something calls your group to prayer, run with it and trust the Spirit. Some world events that have led to spontaneous prayer in my experience are the 9-11 terrorist attacks; the 2004 tsunami that hit many parts of Asia and East Africa; the death of Pope John Paul II; and Hurricanes Katrina, Rita, and Ivan. The teens might be dealing with the death of a coach, supporting a friend who is suffering from cancer, trying to be there for someone who is dealing with an unplanned pregnancy, or perhaps struggling with the transfer of a popular pastor.

Give teens a chance. It is my experience that when I stereotype a group and say, "Oh, these guys can't handle shared prayer," more powerful prayer is born. Do not be afraid to try something new. Shared prayer can mean passing a candle around a circle and giving everyone a chance to pray, but it could also mean starting a youth-group prayer blog where teens are welcome to add their prayers anytime.

Involve Teens in Leading Prayer

Look for opportunities to involve the teens in leading prayer. The prayer services in this book offer many opportunities for them to lead and participate in prayer. We can teach teens that prayer is not a spectator sport by inviting them to get off the bench.

As you model a variety of prayer forms and styles, encourage the teens, with your guidance, to plan and lead their own prayer services.

Prayer Takes Practice

The more you lead prayer with teens, the more comfortable you will become. No one is an expert after a first piano lesson. No one can dunk every basket when first handed a basketball. If you are a little nervous about praying with teens, that is okay. Give it your best, and give it time.

Prayer Brings Balance into Our Lives

Why pray? There are many reasons, each as different as the teens you encounter in your ministry. But as I gift this prayer resource to you and your teens, allow me to share one more illustration . . .

At the end of my Confirmation class on prayer, I ask all the teens to stand on one foot for as long as they can. They may not hold on to anyone or anything, and one foot may not be supported by the other leg. It must stay off the floor. We laugh. They fall down. Some hop. Some get frustrated. Some wave their arms. Some can do it longer. When we are done, I ask, "What can this activity teach us about prayer?"

Some say that prayer takes practice or concentration. Others say prayer requires the support of others. What I hope to share is that prayer helps us keep our life in balance. Like the pole that a tightrope walker uses, a healthy prayer life helps us keep our personal and spiritual life in balance.

This book of prayer is my gift to you. God bless you in your ministry. You can be sure that I am praying for you.

1 Welcoming God and Others

Themes
- All are welcome
- Be open to God and others
- Ask, search, knock

Suggested Uses
- At a youth-group meeting when new members are being welcomed
- As a prayer service for incoming freshmen
- At a youth-group meeting on hospitality or avoiding cliques

Forms of Prayer
- Symbolic prayer
- Scripture
- Music
- Reflection
- Petition
- Traditional prayer
- Liturgical prayer
- Storytelling

Extra Prayer Ideas

A. The Scriptures contain many examples of times when Jesus welcomed those whom no one else would welcome—lepers (see Luke 17:11–19), tax collectors (see Luke 19:1–10), sinners (see John 8:1–11), Samaritans (see John 4:7–30), and even Roman soldiers (see Matthew 8:53). Include one of these Scripture passages in your prayer.

B. Invite the teens to attend the rite of welcome for the catechumens in the RCIA program. The teens could be part of a welcoming reception after the liturgy.

C. Decorate a large jar with the words *Ask, Search,* and *Knock.* Keep it in your gathering space with paper and a pen or pencil nearby. Invite the teens to add petitions to the prayer jar whenever they feel a need.

D. Take time to pray for those who feel lost, lonely, and outcast.

E. Invite an older teen, perhaps a high school senior, to give a witness talk on how it feels to be excluded versus welcomed. The teen could describe a time when he or she felt shunned and a time when he or she felt welcomed and accepted by others.

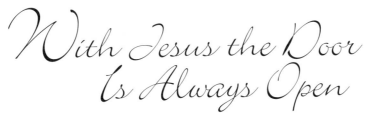

With Jesus the Door Is Always Open

Materials Gather the following items before beginning the prayer service:
- ❑ a sheet of newsprint
- ❑ the song "Seek Ye First," by Karen Lafferty
- ❑ *The Catholic Youth Bible*® or another Bible
- ❑ seven copies of resource 1–A, "Prayers of Petition for Welcoming Others"
- ❑ a wooden or cardboard door on a stand
- ❑ fine-tipped markers
- ❑ a CD of reflective music
- ❑ a CD player

Preparation
- Make a small wooden or cardboard welcome door with a doorknob and a stand for the door. Place the door in a central location where it will be easily seen and accessible. Have markers nearby for the signing ritual.
- Ask several teens to be involved in preparing for the prayer service. Some can work together to choose a Christian rock or contemporary liturgical song to be used in the service.
- Ask one teen to prepare the Scripture reading:
  ○ Luke 11:9 (Ask, Search, Knock)
- Ask seven teens to prepare the petitions on resource 1–A, "Prayers of Petition for Welcoming Others."
- Ask an adult youth leader to prepare a short reflection focused on the Scripture passage or the theme of the prayer service.
- Display on newsprint the following responses:
  ○ "Ask, and it will be given you; search, and you will find; knock, and the door will be opened for you" (Luke 11:9).
  ○ "Lord, help us to be open to you."
  Introduce these responses and explain to the teens how they will use them throughout the prayer service.
- Teach the song "Seek Ye First."

Order of Prayer

Call to Prayer **Prayer Leader:** The door is open. Come in. Meet new people. Stay awhile. Let us open ourselves to Jesus in prayer. We pray for ourselves, our youth group, and our parish community (or school) that we may be open to God and to one another.

Opening Song Invite the teens to sing "Seek Ye First."

Reading   *[Direct the Scripture reader to read Luke 11:9.]*

Prayer Leader: Our response is, "Ask, and it will be given you; search, and you will find; knock, and the door will be opened for you" *[Luke 11:9]*. **All respond.**

Prayer Leader: Please take a few moments to reflect on this question: How would Jesus greet you if you ran into him today? *[Pause for quiet time.]*
[Direct the adult leader to read his or her prepared reflection.]

Prayer Leader: The door is always open; let us pray to be open to God and others. **All respond.**

Prayers of Petition   *[Direct the readers to read their assigned prayers from their copies of resource 1–A, "Prayers of Petition for Welcoming Others."]*

Petition Reader: *Our response is, "Lord, help us to be open to you."* **All Respond.**

Petition Reader: We pray for our Church, as it struggles through difficult times, that the Holy Spirit guide our bishops and priests. We pray to the Lord. We pray for our parish, that we welcome all people—young and old, rich and poor, people of all nationalities—with open arms and hearts. We pray to the Lord. **All Respond.**

Petition Reader: We pray for the senior-high youth group of our parish, that we make everyone feel welcome at every meeting and activity. We pray to the Lord. **All Respond.**

Petition Reader: We pray for all the teens, those present and those who cannot be with us tonight, that they are able to find God in their everyday lives. We pray to the Lord. **All Respond.**

Petition Reader: We pray for all the teens, those present and those who cannot be with us tonight, that they are able to find God in all their relationships. We pray to the Lord. **All Respond.**

Petition Reader: We pray for all the teens that are sick, and all the friends and family that are sick, that God bring them God's healing presence and touch. We pray to the Lord. **All Respond.**

Petition Reader: We pray for all the teens that have recently moved here or are starting at a new school, that they make new friends and feel comfortable in their new environments. We pray to the Lord. **All Respond.**

Petition Reader: "Ask and it will be given you; search, and you will find; knock, and the door will be opened to you" *[Luke 11:9]*.

Signing of the Welcome Door   *[Invite the young people to come forward and sign the welcome door as a promise to be open to God and others. Play a reflective song while the participants are signing the door.]*

Prayer Leader: "Ask, and it will be given you; search, and you will find; knock, and the door will be opened for you" *[Luke 11:9]*.

[Close by leading the group in the Lord's Prayer.]

Prayers of Petition for Welcoming Others

Reader 1   Our response is, "Lord, help us to be open to you." **All Respond.**

Reader 1   We pray for our Church, as it struggles through difficult times, that the Holy Spirit guide our bishops and priests. We pray to the Lord. We pray for our parish, that we welcome all people—young and old, rich and poor, people of all nationalities—with open arms and hearts. We pray to the Lord. **All Respond.**

Reader 2   We pray for the senior-high youth group of our parish, that we make everyone feel welcome at every meeting and activity. We pray to the Lord. **All Respond.**

Reader 3   We pray for all the teens, those present and those who cannot be with us tonight, that they are able to find God in their everyday lives. We pray to the Lord. **All Respond.**

Reader 4   We pray for all the teens, those present and those who cannot be with us tonight, that they are able to find God in all their relationships. We pray to the Lord. **All Respond.**

Reader 5   We pray for all the teens that are sick, and all the friends and family that are sick, that God bring them God's healing presence and touch. We pray to the Lord. **All Respond.**

Reader 6   We pray for all the teens that have recently moved here or are starting at a new school, that they make new friends and feel comfortable in their new environments. We pray to the Lord. **All Respond.**

Reader 7   "Ask, and it will be given you; search, and you will find; knock, and the door will be opened to you" *[Luke 11:9].*

(The scriptural quotation on this resource is from the New Revised Standard Version of the Bible, Catholic Edition. Copyright © 1993 and 1989 by the Division of Christian Education of the National Council of the Churches of Christ in the United States of America. All rights reserved.)

A Commissioning Prayer

Themes
- Living the Gospel
- Being the hands of Jesus
- Christian leadership
- Following Jesus
- Jesus walks with us

Suggested Uses
- For commissioning any leadership or ministerial position for teens or adults
- To start a new youth ministry or school year
- To close a leadership training program

Forms of Prayer
- Symbolic prayer
- Scripture
- Music
- Silent prayer
- Journaling
- Poetry

Extra Prayer Ideas

A. Invite the teens to write their own blessings for special times in their lives, such as getting their drivers' licenses, playing in a playoff game, moving away, and so on.

B. Give the teens some quiet reflection time on the idea drawn from the prayer of Saint Teresa of Ávila, that Jesus has no hands on earth but ours. The teens can write in their journals about ways they can be the hands of Jesus.

C. Have the teens spend some time with each verse of the prayer on resource 2–A, "Prayer with Hands." Challenge them to find a Scripture passage related to each. They can also look for examples of people who need prayer.

D. As the teens leave, give each of them a copy of the poem "Footprints," by Mary Stevenson. This poem is widely available on the Internet.

E. Search the Scriptures for other stories of discipleship and pray about how each of us can follow Jesus with hands and heart.

Come, Follow Me . . . with Hands and Heart

Materials Gather the following items before beginning the prayer service:
- [ ] a pillar candle
- [ ] matches
- [ ] eight pieces of construction paper, each a different color
- [ ] a pair of scissors
- [ ] three copies of THE CATHOLIC YOUTH BIBLE or another Bible
- [ ] eight copies of resource 2–A, "Prayer with Hands"
- [ ] a copy of the CD *The Promise*, by Plus One (Atlantic Records, 2000)
- [ ] a CD player

Preparation
- Ask three teens to prepare the Scripture readings:
  - Matthew 4:18–22 (Jesus Calls the First Disciples)
  - John 1:35–39 (Come and See)
  - Mark 2:3–14 (The Call of Matthew)
- Ask a teen to cut eight handprints out of the construction paper, using all eight colors.
  - Invite eight teens to prepare the prayer on resource 2–A, "Prayer with Hands," and to place their paper handprints around the candle after they read.
- Cue the CD to the song "Written on My Heart."
  - Ask a teen to light the candle at the beginning of prayer.

Order of Prayer

Call to Prayer **Prayer Leader:** The theme for our prayer is Come, Follow Me.

Just as Jesus called the first Apostles to come and follow him, Jesus has called our new youth leaders to follow him. Jesus calls us to follow him as members of our youth group and as part of our parish.

We now join in prayer, asking Jesus for the courage to follow him in our everyday lives and to live the challenge of the Gospel.

Lighting of the Youth-Group Candle Invite the candle lighter to come forward and light the pillar candle.

First Reading Invite the first Scripture reader to read Matthew 4:18–22.
Play the song "Written on My Heart."

Reflection on the Words of Albert Camus **Prayer Leader:** There is a well-known saying attributed to writer Albert Camus that goes like this:

Don't walk in front of me, I may not follow.
Don't walk behind me, I may not lead.
Just walk beside me and be my friend.

If we look at this saying with Jesus in mind, this might be our prayer:
Jesus, walk in front of me as my guide on the way to the Father.
Jesus, walk behind me, so I know I never have to stand alone.
Jesus, walk beside me as my friend. You became like me so I can be more like you.

Second Reading   Invite the second Scripture reader to read John 1:35–39.

Prayer with Hands   **Reader 1:** If I take the hand of Jesus, . . .
he may take me places I really don't want to go.

Reader 2: If I take the hand of Jesus, . . .
he may ask me to care less about stuff and more about people.

Reader 3: If I take the hand of Jesus, . . .
he may ask me to do what is right and not just what is popular.

Reader 4: If I take the hand of Jesus, . . .
he may ask me to reach out to people whom no one else really cares about.

Reader 5: If I take the hand of Jesus, . . .
he may ask me to be the first one who refuses to keep on fighting.

Reader 6: If I take the hand of Jesus, . . .
he may ask me to be last so that another can be first.

Reader 7: If I take the hand of Jesus, . . .
I may learn to see with my heart and not just my eyes.

Reader 8: If I take the hand of Jesus, . . .
nothing will ever be the same.

Leader: Let us pause silently to share with Jesus the prayers in our hearts right now.

Silent Prayer   *[Allow a minute or two of quiet time for the teens to pray silently.]*

Third Reading   Invite the third Scripture reader to read Mark 2:3–14.

Blessing   **Prayer Leader:** Please extend your hand in blessing toward someone near you and repeat after me *[Pause after each line of the prayer to allow the teens to repeat.]*:
May God bless you
as you go on your way
and give you courage
to live the Gospel every day.
In the name of the Father, and of the Son, and of the Holy Spirit.
Amen.

Prayer with Hands

Reader 1   If I take the hand of Jesus . . .
he may take me places I really don't want to go.

Reader 2   If I take the hand of Jesus . . .
he may ask me to care less about stuff and more about people.

Reader 3   If I take the hand of Jesus, . . .
he may ask me to do what is right and not just what is popular.

Reader 4   If I take the hand of Jesus, . . .
he may ask me to reach out to people whom no one else really cares about.

Reader 5   If I take the hand of Jesus, . . .
he may ask me to be the first one who refuses to keep on fighting.

Reader 6   If I take the hand of Jesus, . . .
he may ask me to be last so that another can be first.

Reader 7   If I take the hand of Jesus, . . .
I may learn to see with my heart and not just my eyes.

Reader 8   If I take the hand of Jesus, . . .
nothing will ever be the same.

3 Images of Discipleship

Themes
- Being light and salt
- Jesus is light
- Walking in the light
- Proclaiming the Gospel
- Making a difference

Suggested Uses
- As an opening or closing prayer for a multi-parish event
- At a youth rally
- As an affirmation
- At the start of a new school year

Forms of Prayer
- Symbolic prayer
- Scripture
- Drama-dialogue-mime
- Litany
- Music
- Silent prayer
- Journaling
- Reflection
- Shared prayer

Extra Prayer Ideas

A. Help the teens understand the images of salt and light. Pass a salt shaker around the circle, and ask each teen to name one way he or she can be salt for the world. Pass a candle around the circle, and ask each teen to name one way he or she can be light for the world.

B. Each day for a week, invite the teens to look for ways they can be the light of Christ in their world and to write their experiences in their prayer journal.

C. Start a discussion about how one flame can pierce the darkness and how it takes courage to be the first ray of light. Challenge the teens to think of ways they can be many flames working together to make a difference.

You Are Salt and Light

Materials Gather the following items before beginning the prayer service:
- ❑ seven copies of *THE CATHOLIC YOUTH BIBLE* or another Bible
- ❑ an Easter candle
- ❑ six pillar candles
- ❑ matches
- ❑ one copy of resource 3–A, "Litany of Light"
- ❑ the song "Cry the Gospel," by Tom Booth
- ❑ two copies of resource 3–B, "Salty Dialogue"
- ❑ the song "Go Make a Difference," by Steve Angrisano

Preparation
- Invite six teens to prepare the Scripture readings:
  - Genesis 1:1–4 (Creation of Light)
  - John 8:12 (Jesus the Light of the World)
  - John 12:46 (Jesus Comes as Light)
  - Ephesians 5:8 (Now You Are Light)
  - 1 John 1:5 (God Is Light)
  - Matthew 5:14–15 (You Are the Light of the World)
- Invite six teens to hold the pillar candles. Give each teen some matches, or assign another teen to light the candles as the teens stand.
- Ask a teen to lead the litany on resource 3–A, "Litany of Light."
- Choose two teens to prepare to read the script on resource 3–B, "Salty Dialogue."
- Ask a teen to prepare the closing Scripture passage:
  - Matthew 5:14–16 (You Are the Light of the World)
- Teach the songs "Cry the Gospel" and "Go Make a Difference."
- Light the Easter candle and darken the prayer space.

Order of Prayer

The Light of the Scriptures As each teen reads his or her Scripture passage, he or she stands up, lights a candle, and holds the candle up for all to see. As the last teen lights his or her candle, turn on the lights in the prayer space.

Invite the first reader to read Genesis 1:1–4.

Invite the second reader to read John 8:12.

Invite the third reader to read John 12:46.

Invite the fourth reader to read Ephesians 5:8.

Invite the fifth reader to read 1 John 1:5.

Invite the sixth reader to read Matthew 5:14–15.

Litany of Light   **Litany Leader:** Our response is, "Let us be light." **All respond.**

[Pause for all to respond after each line of the litany.]

Litany Leader: When darkness fills our thoughts . . .
  When darkness fills our hearts . . .
  When darkness touches our friends . . .
  When darkness touches our schools . . .
  When darkness touches our parish . . .
  When darkness touches our work . . .
  When darkness touches our teams . . .
  When darkness touches our community . . .
  When darkness touches our nation . . .
  When darkness fills our world . . .

[Invite the teens to sing verse one and the chorus of "Cry the Gospel."]

Salty Dialogue   *[Invite the dialogue readers to position themselves on either side of the prayer space, facing each other but in view of the entire group.]*

Reader 1: *You are the salt of the earth.*

Reader 2: What kind of compliment is that?

Reader 1: It means you are full of life, zest, flavor.

Reader 2: You have got to be kidding. Salt is worthless. It isn't even worth a few pennies.

Reader 1: Ever try eating things without salt, like french fries? Salt adds a lot of flavor to everything we eat.

Reader 2: Oh, yeah, well you can rub salt in wounds, too, and it can really hurt.

Reader 1: Well, sometimes we need to be salty, like pointing out when things are not right and we need to take a stand for what we believe.

Reader 2: The only thing salt is good for is throwing on the road in the winter.

Reader 1: But salt is good for melting icy hearts too. We can change the way people treat one another, even change the world.

Reader 2: By being salt for the earth?

Reader 1: And by making sure we do not lose our flavor.

Reader 2: Hmm . . .

Reader 1: Did you know that Jesus calls each us to be salt for the earth?

Reader 2: No, but I am sure you are going to tell me.

Reader 1: Jesus calls us to add flavor to our lives and the lives of others by preaching the Gospel, the Good News, to everyone we meet.

Reader 2: *[Looking out and addressing the whole group]* Are you salt for the earth?

Reader 1: We can be salt in the wounds of oppressors and those who do evil in the world by calling for an end to war and speaking out for those who are poor, sick, or lonely.

Reader 2: *[Looking out and addressing the whole group]* Are you salt for the earth?

Reader 1: We can melt icy hearts by calling for understanding and dialogue among races and countries, among families, and even among different religions.

Reader 2: *[Looking out and addressing the whole group]* Are you salt for the earth?

[Invite the teens to sing verse two and the chorus of "Cry the Gospel."]

Silent Prayer   **Prayer Leader:** Let us pray for all the teens gathered here and all the teens of *[name of parish or school]* that each day we can become more like what Christ asks us to be—light for all the world and salt for all the earth.

[Pause for reflection.]

Closing Reading and Blessing   Invite the last Scripture reader to read Matthew 5:14–16.

Closing Song   Invite the teens to sing "Go Make a Difference."

Litany of Light

Litany Leader Our response is, "Let us be light." All respond.

[Pause for all to respond after each line of the litany.]

Litany Leader When darkness fills our thoughts . . .

When darkness fills our hearts . . .

When darkness touches our friends . . .

When darkness touches our schools . . .

When darkness touches our parish . . .

When darkness touches our work . . .

When darkness touches our teams . . .

When darkness touches our community . . .

When darkness touches our nation . . .

When darkness fills our world . . .

Salty Dialogue

[Readers should position themselves on either side of the prayer space, facing each other but in view of the entire group.]

Reader 1 You are the salt of the earth.

Reader 2 What kind of compliment is that?

Reader 1 It means you are full of life, zest, flavor.

Reader 2 You have got to be kidding. Salt is worthless. It isn't even worth a few pennies.

Reader 1 Ever try eating things without salt, like french fries? Salt adds a lot of flavor to everything we eat.

Reader 2 Oh, yeah, well you can rub salt in wounds, too, and it can really hurt.

Reader 1 Well, sometimes we need to be salty, like pointing out when things are not right and we need to take a stand for what we believe.

Reader 2 The only thing salt is good for is throwing on the road in the winter.

Reader 1 But salt is good for melting icy hearts too. We can change the way people treat one another, even change the world.

Reader 2 By being salt for the earth?

Reader 1 And by making sure we do not lose our flavor.

Reader 2 Hmm. . .

Reader 1 Did you know that Jesus calls each us to be salt for the earth?

Reader 2 No, but I am sure you are going to tell me.

Reader 1 Jesus calls us to add flavor to our lives and the lives of others by preaching the Gospel, the Good News, to everyone we meet.

Reader 2 *[Looking out and addressing the whole group]* Are you salt for the earth?

Reader 1 We can be salt in the wounds of oppressors and those who do evil in the world by calling for an end to war and speaking out for those who are poor, sick, or lonely.

Reader 2 *[Looking out and addressing the whole group]* Are you salt for the earth?

Reader 1 We can melt icy hearts by calling for understanding and dialogue among races and countries, among families, and even among different religions.

Reader 2 *[Looking out and addressing the whole group]* Are you salt for the earth?

Making Time for Jesus

Themes
- Listening for your call
- Answering the call
- Stop making excuses!
- Following Christ

Suggested Uses
- At a youth-group meeting on discipleship
- During a class or youth-group meeting during Lent
- During a youth leadership weekend

Forms of Prayer
- Scripture
- Symbolic prayer
- Reflection
- Music
- Silent prayer
- Journaling

Extra Prayer Ideas
A. Talk about ways your group can "put its best foot forward" in sharing the Gospel message of Jesus.
B. Divide the large group into pairs and have the partners take each other on a blindfolded trust walk. Ask them to end their walk at the foot of the cross. Invite them to share how we need to lead others to Jesus.
C. Invite the teens to find examples in the Scriptures of ways Jesus calls us to follow him. Challenge them to implement one of the ways into their daily life.

Placing Our Feet at the Foot of the Cross

Materials   Gather the following items before beginning the prayer service:
- ❑ brown paper bags, one for each teen
- ❑ several pairs of scissors
- ❑ pens or pencils, one for each teen
- ❑ the youth-group candle from chapter 2
- ❑ matches
- ❑ two copies of THE CATHOLIC YOUTH BIBLE or another Bible
- ❑ two copies of resource 4–A, "Voices"
- ❑ a cross to display in the prayer space
- ❑ the song "I Will Choose Christ," by Tom Booth

Preparation
- Ask two teens to prepare the Scripture readings:
  - ○ Matthew 19:16–22 (The Rich Young Man)
  - ○ Matthew 4:18–20 (The Disciples Left Everything Behind and Followed Jesus)
- Ask two teens to read the voices on resource 4–A, "Voices."
- Invite a teen to light the youth-group candle at the beginning of the prayer.
- Teach the song "I Will Choose Christ."
- Place the cross and the youth-group candle in the center of the prayer space.
- As the teens arrive, invite them to trace one of their feet on a brown paper bag, cut out the footprint, and take the footprint and a pen or pencil into the prayer space.

Order of Prayer

Call to Prayer   **Prayer Leader:** We begin our prayer, as we begin all things, in the name of the Father, and of the Son, and of the Holy Spirit.

[Instruct the candle lighter to light the youth-group candle.]

First Reading   **Prayer Leader:** And Jesus said, "Come, follow me" *[Matthew 19:21]*.

[Invite the first Scripture reader to read Matthew 19:16-22.]

Prayer Leader: And Jesus said, "Come, follow me."

Reflection   **Prayer Leader:** In silence, think about your personal answers to these questions:
- The young man couldn't give up his riches. What riches do you need to give up to follow Jesus?
- How do you fail to make time for Jesus?
- What excuses do you make for not creating time for Jesus?

Voices   **Voice 1:** I'll come when the game is over.

Voice 2: I'll come after I'm done talking on the phone.

Voice 1: I'll come after I come home from the mall.

Voice 2: I'll come after my favorite show is over.

Voice 1: I'll come after I sign off the Internet.

Voice 2: I'll come when things are better in my life.

Voice 1: I'll come when I'm in real in trouble and need your help.

[Invite the teens to take a few moments to think about the excuses they make for not creating time for Jesus.]

Prayer Leader: And Jesus said, "Come, follow me."

Second Reading   *[Direct the second Scripture reader to read Matthew 4:18–20.]*

Prayer Leader: And Jesus said, "Come, follow me."

Footprint Prayers   *[Ask the teens to write a personal prayer to Jesus on their footprints. Invite them to reflect on their call to follow Jesus and write a prayer from the heart. When they are finished, ask them to place their footprints at the foot of the cross.]*

[Direct the teens to sing "I Will Choose Christ."]

Prayer Leader: And Jesus said, "Come, follow me." I'll come after I'm done talking on the phone.

Voices

Voice 1	I'll come when the game is over.
Voice 2	I'll come after I'm done talking on the phone.
Voice 1	I'll come after I come home from the mall.
Voice 2	I'll come after my favorite show is over.
Voice 1	I'll come after I sign off the Internet.
Voice 2	I'll come when things are better in my life.
Voice 1	I'll come when I'm in real in trouble and need your help.

5 Walking with the Poor

Themes
- Walking in the shoes of another
- Empathizing with those in need
- Praying for peace and justice
- Stepping outside of ourselves

Suggested Uses
- In a class on Catholic social teaching
- On a mission trip
- As a morning prayer on a peace and justice retreat
- For a Christian leadership program

Forms of Prayer
- Scripture
- Reflection
- Music
- Shared prayer
- Symbolic prayer
- Petition

Extra Prayer Ideas
A. Invite the teens to pray the stations of the cross in bare feet or stocking feet.
B. Imagine the type of sandals Jesus wore. What were they like? What can they tell us about the simple carpenter?
C. Ask the teens to reflect on Matthew 25:31–46. How does this Scripture reading relate to the saying "Do not judge your brother until you have walked a mile in his moccasins"?
D. Ask the teens to count the number of shoes and boots in their closets at home. Challenge them to donate a certain amount of money or time for every pair they own. Suggest that every time they put their shoes on, they pray for those who are poor.

In Jesus's Shoes

Materials   Gather the following items before beginning the prayer service:
- ❑ pillar candles, one for each group of six to eight
- ❑ matches for each group of six to eight
- ❑ a CD of reflective music
- ❑ a CD player
- ❑ a copy of the CD *Big Tent Revival Greatest Hits*, by Big Tent Revival (Ardent Records, 2002)
- ❑ one copy of resource 5–A, "Walking in Jesus's Shoes"
- ❑ THE CATHOLIC YOUTH BIBLE or another Bible
- ❑ eight copies of resource 5–B, "Prayers of Petition for Those That Are Poor"
- ❑ pens or pencils
- ❑ small pieces of paper in the shape of a shoe
- ❑ safety pins, one for each teen

Preparation
- • Place the pillar candles where the small groups of teens will be sitting on the floor.
- • Ask one teen to prepare the Scripture reading:
  - ○ John 13:3–5,12–15 (Jesus Washes the Disciples' Feet)
- • Ask one teen to prepare the reflection on resource 5–A, "Walking in Jesus's Shoes"
- • Ask eight teens to prepare the prayer on resource 5–B, "Prayers of Petition for Those That Are Poor."
- • Have quiet music playing as the teens enter the prayer space.
- • As the teens enter, ask them to take off their shoes and leave them outside the prayer space.
- • Invite the teens to sit in close circles with their small groups.

Order of Prayer

Call to Prayer   **Prayer Leader:** We are called to proclaim God's justice and to strive to change the causes of oppression and poverty. We must witness the Gospel in a world of excess, wealth, and selfishness. We are called especially to promote the dignity of the poor. We must make a radical response to Christ and be daring in the ways we reach out to those in need.

Opening Song   Play the song "What Would Jesus Do?" from the *Big Tent Revival Greatest Hits* CD.

Reflection

Reflection Leader:

Imagine walking in Jesus's shoes (or sandals),
talking to a Samaritan woman,
healing someone on the Sabbath,
walking on water,
tossing money changers out of the Temple,
standing up to the Pharisees,
reaching out to lepers,
urging people to love their enemies,
telling people, "Blessed are those who are persecuted" *[Matthew 5:10].*
We have some pretty big shoes to fill!

Reading

Direct the Scripture reader to read John 13:3–5,12–15.

Prayers of Petition

Prayer Leader: The Gospel calls us to be hope for those who are poor. Let us listen to the voices of teens, in our country and throughout the world, that desperately need hope. Let us add our prayers to their voices. Our response is, "We will love you and pray for you." **All respond.**

Voice 1: My name is Josef. I have lived my whole life in a country torn apart by war. I am always afraid. I can only dream of what it must be like to be at peace. Please pray for me, my sisters and brothers. **All respond.**

Voice 2: My name is Miguel. A hurricane came through and destroyed our island. There is nothing left where my home once stood. I can't even find some of my friends. Please pray for me, my brothers and sisters. **All respond.**

Voice 3: My name is Sanche. Our land has been without rain for a long time. Nothing grows here anymore. We sometimes go for days without anything to eat. And many of us are dying. Please pray for us, my sisters and brothers. **All respond.**

Voice 4: My name is Anna, but you will never meet me. I will never get to live a life like yours and see the pain and joy of being a teenager. My mother decided to have an abortion. Please pray for me, my brothers and sisters. **All respond.**

Voice 5: My name is Matthew. It all started at a party where everyone was trying cocaine. I never thought I could get addicted. Now all I think about every minute is getting more coke. Please pray for me, my sisters and brothers. **All respond.**

Voice 6: My name is Andrew. My parents are going through a divorce. All they do is fight and blame me for everything. I feel like I am torn apart. I want it all to end. Please pray for me, my brothers and sisters. **All respond.**

Voice 7: My name is Kristin. I ran away from home when I was twelve, and I have lived on the street for two years. Most of the time I am hungry, cold, and scared. I wonder if I can ever go home again. Please pray for me, my sisters and brothers. **All respond.**

Voice 8: My name is Jean. I am really frightened about growing up when I see all the awful things that are going on in the world. It is almost as if people have forgotten all about God. Please pray for all of us, my brothers and sisters. **All respond.**

Prayer Leader: Sisters and brothers, we offer these prayers to our Lord Jesus, who not only calls us to hope but also to help build a just and peaceful world. We offer these prayers of hope in the name of the risen Lord. Amen.

Small-Group Prayer

Prayer Leader: I invite you now to think about someone who is poor, sick, lonely, scared, beaten, neglected, abused, or helpless. The person could be someone you have met and perhaps know by name or face, or it could be someone you have never met but want to pray for.

Share with others in your group the person you would like to pray for. Invite them to walk in the shoes of that person for a few moments and share with your group what the person might be going through.

[Distribute the pens or pencils, the pieces of paper in the shape of a shoe, and the safety pins.] After you pray for that person, write his or her name (or a simple description, such as "homeless woman") on your shoe intention slip. Say the following prayer: "I will keep you in my prayers and close to my heart." Then pin the intention over your heart.

When each person in your group has had a chance to share his or her story and prayer, gather your shoes and leave quietly.

Walking in Jesus's Shoes

Imagine walking in Jesus's shoes (or sandals),
talking to a Samaritan woman,
healing someone on the Sabbath,
walking on water,
tossing money changers out of the Temple,
standing up to the Pharisees,
reaching out to lepers,
urging people to love their enemies,
telling people, "Blessed are those who are persecuted" *[Matthew 5:10]*.
We have some pretty big shoes to fill!

Prayers of Petition for Those That Are Poor

Prayer Leader   The Gospel calls us to be hope for those who are poor. Let us listen to the voices of teens, in our country and throughout the world, that desperately need hope. Let us add our prayers to their voices. Our response is, "We will love you and pray for you." **All respond.**

Voice 1   My name is Josef. I have lived my whole life in a country torn apart by war. I am always afraid. I can only dream of what it must be like to be at peace. Please pray for me, my sisters and brothers. **All respond.**

Voice 2   My name is Miguel. A hurricane came through and destroyed our island. There is nothing left where my home once stood. I can't even find some of my friends. Please pray for me, my brothers and sisters. **All respond.**

Voice 3   My name is Sanche. Our land has been without rain for a long time. Nothing grows here anymore. We sometimes go for days without anything to eat. And many of us are dying. Please pray for us, my sisters and brothers. **All respond.**

Voice 4   My name is Anna, but you will never meet me. I will never get to live a life like yours and see the pain and joy of being a teenager. My mother decided to have an abortion. Please pray for me, my brothers and sisters. **All respond.**

Voice 5   My name is Matthew. It all started at a party where everyone was trying cocaine. I never thought I could get addicted. Now all I think about every minute is getting more coke. Please pray for me, my sisters and brothers. **All respond.**

Voice 6   My name is Andrew. My parents are going through a divorce. All they do is fight and blame me for everything. I feel like I am torn apart. I want it all to end. Please pray for me, my brothers and sisters. **All respond.**

Voice 7   My name is Kristin. I ran away from home when I was twelve, and I have lived on the street for two years. Most of the time I am hungry, cold, and scared. I wonder if I can ever go home again. Please pray for me, my sisters and brothers. **All respond.**

Voice 8   Sisters and brothers, we offer these prayers to our Lord Jesus, who not only calls us to hope but also to help build a just and peaceful world. We offer these prayers of hope in the name of the risen Lord. Amen.

6 Prayer for Justice and Peace

Themes
- Making a difference
- Recognizing the power of one
- Standing up for what is right
- Living justly

Suggested Uses
- Before a meeting or class on social-justice issues
- To commission a group embarking on a service project
- At the start of a work camp
- As affirmation for youth
- As part of a leadership training program
- To celebrate All Saints' Day

Forms of Prayer
- Symbolic prayer
- Storytelling
- Affirmation
- Art
- Journaling
- Scripture
- Shared prayer

Extra Prayer Ideas

A. Ask each teen to choose one of the people from the prayer in this prayer service and learn more about his or her life. After they have researched the person's life, have the teens write a prayer in response to what they learned.

B. Celebrate the teens in your community who have made a difference in the lives of others. Acknowledge them at the end of Mass one weekend or in the parish newsletter.

C. Ask the teens to clip out newspaper stories about social-justice issues. Invite them to write an original prayer inspired by what they read.

D. Start a discussion about what makes it tough to stand up for what is right. Ask the teens to search the Scriptures for examples of Jesus's standing up for what is right.

E. Introduce the teens to the seven key Catholic social-justice teachings. Make individual posters for each one, and be sure each poster includes a title, a synopsis, local action keys, and prayers written by the teens.

F. Work with the teens to create an entire prayer service patterned after the nameless, faceless character presented by voice 7 on resource 6–A, "Voices of the Just." Each prayer could focus on a different social injustice within society.

Standing with Others Who Made a Difference

Materials Gather the following items before beginning the prayer service:
- ❑ a pillar candle (the candle of hope)
- ❑ matches
- ❑ seven copies of resource 6–A, "Voices of the Just"
- ❑ copies of handout 6–A, "Standing with Others Who Made a Difference: Concluding Prayer," one for each teen

Preparation
- Ask seven teens to prepare the voice parts on resource 6–A, "Voices of the Just"
- Invite a teen to light the pillar candle, which in this prayer is called the candle of hope.

Order of Prayer

[Invite the candle lighter to light the candle of hope.]

Call to Prayer **Prayer Leader:** Today we gather in prayer to thank God for the gift of Jesus and his inspiration to us to take a stand and make a difference in the world. We pray for courage to follow his example in our everyday lives. We now join in prayer with those who have gone before and stood up for what is right and good.

[Invite each reader to stand to read his or her role and remain standing as the prayer continues.]

Voices of the Just **Voice 1:** My name is Mother Teresa. I worked with the poorest of the poor in India, the outcasts, the people no one cared about and would never touch. Like Saint Teresa of Ávila, I believe that Jesus has no hands but our own. Won't you reach out to the poor with me?

Voice 2: My name is Dorothy Day. I founded Catholic Worker House, which provided a haven for the poor and needy. I championed the rights of the worker to a just wage. I believe that social change can be achieved only through nonviolence. Won't you work for change with me?

Voice 3: My name is Archbishop Romero. I led the Church in El Salvador and worked tirelessly to bring social justice to my country. I tried to end government violence against the poor. My stands made me very unpopular. I was assassinated while saying Mass in March of 1980. Won't you stand against violence with me?

Voice 4: My name is Maximilian Kolbe. I am a Polish Franciscan priest who was imprisoned during World War II in Auschwitz, a Nazi concentration camp. I volunteered to take the place of a young father condemned to starve to death. Won't you place the needs of others before yourself?

Voice 5: My name is Sr. Thea Bowman. I am a singer, an evangelist, and a member of the Franciscan Sisters of Perpetual Adoration. I am a champion of African American culture. I didn't let cancer stop me from speaking and singing out about what is right. Won't you offer hope and courage to others?

Voice 6: My name is Cardinal Bernardin. I led the Archdiocese of Chicago and chaired the U.S. Bishops' committee that drafted a pastoral letter on war and peace. I was a constant defender of the sanctity and dignity of human life from conception to death. Won't you stand up for right to life with me?

Voice 7: I am the nameless, faceless person who suffers daily at the hands of others. I am the person who needs your love and compassion. I am the sick, the imprisoned, and the babies who will never be born. I am the old, the young, and the poorest of the poor. I am the people who yearn for peace and still hope for justice. I am Jesus. Won't you stand with me?

Concluding   *[Distribute copies of handout 6–A, "Standing with Others Who Made a Difference: Concluding Prayer." Ask all the teens to stand.]*

Prayer Leader: Let us pray.

All:
Loving God, you created us as a gift for each other.
Give us eyes to see all people in need and the injustice in our world.
Give us ears to hear people who call for help.
Give us willing arms to reach out and touch others who need to feel your presence.
Most of all, give us courage to stand up for others and for what we believe.
We ask this through Christ Our Lord.
Amen.

Voices of the Just

[Stand to read your role. Remain standing as the prayer continues.]

Voice 1 My name is Mother Teresa. I worked with the poorest of the poor in India, the outcasts, the people no one cared about and would never touch. Like Saint Teresa of Ávila, I believe that Jesus has no hands but our own. Won't you reach out to the poor with me?

Voice 2 My name is Dorothy Day. I founded the Catholic Worker House, which provided a haven for the poor and needy. I championed the rights of the worker to a just wage. I believe that social change can be achieved only through nonviolence. Won't you work for change with me?

Voice 3 My name is Archbishop Romero. I led the Church in El Salvador and worked tirelessly to bring social justice to my country. I tried to end government violence against the poor. My stands made me very unpopular. I was assassinated while saying Mass in March of 1980. Won't you stand against violence with me?

Voice 4 My name is Maximilian Kolbe. I am a Polish Franciscan priest who was imprisoned during World War II in Auschwitz, a Nazi concentration camp. I volunteered to take the place of a young father condemned to starve to death. Won't you place the needs of others before yourself?

Voice 5 My name is Sr. Thea Bowman. I am a singer, an evangelist, and a member of the Franciscan Sisters of Perpetual Adoration. I am a champion of African American culture. I didn't let cancer stop me from speaking and singing out about what is right. Won't you offer hope and courage to others?

Voice 6 My name is Cardinal Bernardin. I led the Archdiocese of Chicago and chaired the U.S. Bishops' committee that drafted a pastoral letter on war and peace. I was a constant defender of the sanctity and dignity of human life from conception to death. Won't you stand up for right to life with me?

Voice 7 I am the nameless, faceless person who suffers daily at the hands of others. I am the person who needs your love and compassion. I am the sick, the imprisoned, and the babies who will never be born. I am the old, the young, and the poorest of the poor. I am the people who yearn for peace and still hope for justice. I am Jesus. Won't you stand with me?

Standing with Others Who Made a Difference: Concluding Prayer

Prayer Leader   Let us pray.

All   Loving God, you created us as a gift for each other.
Give us eyes to see all people in need and the injustice in our world.
Give us ears to hear people who call for help.
Give us willing arms to reach out and touch others who need to feel your presence.
Most of all, give us courage to stand up for others and for what we believe.
We ask this through Christ Our Lord.
Amen.

7

Faith Like a Child

Themes
- Using your imagination in prayer
- Keeping a sense of wonder
- Looking for God in everyone and everything
- Jesus's calling us to have faith like a child

Suggested Uses
- To help teens broaden their image of God
- To encourage a creative approach to prayer
- To emphasize that relationship with God must continue to grow
- As part of training for teens working with children

Forms of Prayer
- Art
- Shared prayer
- Symbolic prayer
- Drama-dialogue-mime
- Scripture
- Liturgical prayer
- Reflection

Extra Prayer Ideas
A. Instead of using finger paint, use play dough for creating images of God.
B. Instead of using toys, ask the teens to list children's games, such as Duck, Duck, Goose; Follow the Leader; and Simon Says. Have each group pick one game and then discuss what they can learn about God from that game.
C. If your parish has a children's liturgy program, ask the leaders of that program if the teens can serve as assistants and prepare a blessing for the children. Encourage the teens to listen as the children talk about God. They will be surprised at how much they learn from the children.
D. Write the following questions on thin strips of paper and attach each one to a lollipop. Invite teens to enjoy the discussion and the lollipops.
   - What is the first prayer you ever learned?
   - Who taught you about God when you were little?
   - What was your favorite Bible story when you were little?
   - What do you remember about your first Communion?
   - How can you help children get closer to Jesus?
   - Share a childhood memory about church.
   - How did you view God when you were little?
   - What was your favorite song about God?
   - Are there any children in your life right now who teach you about God?
E. Conduct a "scavenger hunt for God," either indoors or outdoors. Gather the teens together and give them very few instructions. Tell them they have five minutes to find God. When time is up, gather the group and ask the teens, one at a time, to share how they found God. Some will find God in nature, pictures, signs, and symbols. Others will find God in one another.

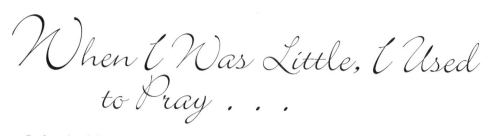
When I Was Little, I Used to Pray . . .

Materials Gather the following items before beginning the prayer service:
- ❑ finger paint
- ❑ sheets of paper for painting on, one for each teen
- ❑ newspaper
- ❑ aluminum pie tins, enough for each color of paint you have
- ❑ sponges, water, and paper towels for cleanup
- ❑ THE CATHOLIC YOUTH BIBLE or another Bible
- ❑ an assortment of small children's toys

Preparation
- Cover the painting area with newspaper to make cleanup easier. Pour a small amount of finger paint into each pie tin.
- Ask the teens to roll up their sleeves and take off any rings.
- Ask one teen to prepare the Scripture reading:
  - Mark 10:13–16 (Jesus Calls Us to Have Faith Like a Child)
- Ask one or more teens to prepare a three-minute skit dramatizing typical ways that children of different ages might pray.
- Poll the group to choose a children's song that most of the teens know, such as "Jesus Loves the Little Children" or "Jesus Loves Me." Practice the first verse.

Order of Prayer

A Child's View of God

Prayer Leader: Try to think back to when you were a young child. How did you view God? What was your image of God?

I invite you now to go to a finger paint station and return to your childhood days. Use the finger paint to create the image of God you held when you were a child.

[When everyone is finished, tell them to leave their paintings to dry and wash their hands. Then divide the large group into small groups of four.]

Prayer Leader: Please discuss the following questions in your small groups:
- What image of God did you draw?
- How has your image of God changed since that time?
- How does your image of God need to change in the future?

[When the small groups have finished discussing, continue with the prayer service.]

Prayer Leader: I encourage you to grow constantly in the way you view God, to continue to grow in your relationship with God, and to continue growing in your faith.

A Chance to Play for God

Prayer Leader: We can find God in all sorts of places and in all sorts of things. When we were young children, we loved to play games; we loved to play with toys. We were good at using our imagination, and we gave it a lot of exercise. When we get older, we sometimes put our imagination in a box. Sometimes we even put God in a box. During this part of the prayer, I challenge you to find God in children's toys.

[Ask each group of four to choose a toy from the center of your prayer space.]

Prayer Leader: As a group, play with the toy you have chosen and then answer this question: What can we learn about God from this toy? Please select a spokesperson to share your group's answers with the large group.

[When they all groups have shared, continue with the prayer service.]

Prayer Leader: I encourage you to look for God everywhere and in everything. Never lose your imagination and never lose your sense of wonder.

Skit

[Invite the teen or teens to come forward to present the skit that dramatizes typical ways that children of different ages might pray. Allow 3 minutes for the skit.]

Scripture Reading

[Direct the Scripture reader to read Mark 10:13–16.]

Prayer Leader: Reflect on the readings by silently answering the following questions:
- What does Jesus mean when he tells us we must have faith like a child?
- How did we pray when we were little?
- How should we pray now?

[Close with the first verse of the children's song that the group practiced before the prayer service.]

8

Prayer Service for Leaders

Themes
- The Lord looks into our hearts
- Learning from experience
- Reflecting on change
- The Gospel colors our life

Suggested Uses
- At a regional gathering of youth ministers or peer ministers
- At a training session or retreat for your youth ministry or peer ministry team

Forms of Prayer
- Music
- Symbolic prayer
- Storytelling
- Meditation
- Reflection

Extra Prayer Ideas

A. Ask the participants to look through a kaleidoscope. Invite them to reflect on how each movement of the lens creates a beautiful change. Challenge them to pray for the courage to look for the beautiful possibilities in life's changes.

B. Ask the participants to reflect on how people and events might look differently if we look at them through the lens of the Gospel.

C. Invite the teen peer leaders to create affirmations or slogans about their ministry based on popular advertisements. An example might be "Peer Ministry: I'm lovin' it!" The teens can print these slogans on T-shirts, or on affirmation cards to post at home or in their school lockers.

Looking Through Different Lenses

Materials

Gather the following items before beginning the prayer service:

☐ the song "Hear Our Prayer," by Tom Tomaszek

☐ THE CATHOLIC YOUTH BIBLE or another Bible

☐ a bowl filled halfway with water

☐ small kaleidoscopes, one for each participant

☐ copies of handout 8–A, "Looking Through the Lens of the Gospel," one for each participant

Preparation

- Teach the song "Hear Our Prayer."
- Ask a participant to prepare the Scripture reading:
  ○ 1 Samuel 16:1,6–7 (God Does Not See As We See)
- Ask a veteran youth minister or peer minister to prepare a short storytelling witness about some experiences that have positively colored his or her ministerial perspective.

Order of Prayer

Opening Song

Invite the participants to sing "Hear Our Prayer."

Call to Prayer

Invite the Scripture reader to read 1 Samuel 16:1,6–7.

Looking Through Tired Eyes

Prayer Leader: Sometimes we look through tired eyes. Look at the bowl of water and silently answer these questions:

- How would you describe the bowl? What words would you use?
- Is the bowl half full or half empty?
- Is your ministry half full or half empty?

[Distribute the kaleidoscopes to the participants.] Look through your kaleidoscope and silently name a difficult time that has colored how you look at your ministry.

Looking Through the Lens of Experience

Prayer Leader: Sometimes the lens of experience colors the way we look at our ministry. Listen to a story from *[speaker's name]*.

[Invite the youth minister or peer minister to share some experiences that have positively colored his or her ministerial perspective.]

Prayer Leader: Look through your kaleidoscope and silently name an experience that colors how you look at your ministry.

Looking Through the Lens of Change

Prayer Leader: We may find that we need to look through the lens of change. Close your eyes for a moment. Imagine that you are sitting near a small reflecting pool. All is still and quiet. There is no breeze, no wind. There is no movement at all. You see only your reflection in the water. All is tranquil. Suddenly, someone tosses a stone into the water. The water ripples, moves, and changes. Your reflection jumps, moves, and changes. For a while, you cannot see yourself. Yet, after a while, the stillness returns. You can see a reflection of yourself again. Open your eyes. Look through your kaleidoscope and silently name a major change in your life. How has it colored the way you look at your ministry?

Looking Through the Lens of the Gospel

[Distribute copies of handout 8–A, "Looking Through the Lens of the Gospel."]

All: If we look through the lens of the Gospel, we may have to force ourselves to see things we do not want to see.
We might have to accept the people who do not do ministry "our way." We might learn to love the pastor or the bishop who just drives us crazy.

We might have to stop gathering mobs of teens and calling it ministry, and instead invite teens to a one-on-one relationship with Jesus.

We might have to seek out the disenfranchised kids, not just the "good" kids.

We might have to love the killers, not just those who have been killed.

Prayer Leader: Look through your kaleidoscope and silently name a way you have failed to let the Gospel color your ministry.

Concluding

Prayer Leader: If we allow God to color our ministry, it will be like looking through a kaleidoscope—ever changing, ever beautiful. We will see the pattern of the kaleidoscope only when we look through the lens. When we learn to see through God's eyes, we will see God's amazing, wondrous grace. As God said to the prophet Samuel, "For the Lord does not see as mortals see; they look on the outward appearance, but the Lord looks on the heart" *[1 Samuel 16:7]*. Amen.

Looking Through the Lens of the Gospel

All If we look through the lens of the Gospel, we may have to force ourselves to see things we do not want to see.

We might have to accept the people who do not do ministry "our way." We might learn to love the pastor or the bishop who just drives us crazy.

We might have to stop gathering mobs of teens and calling it ministry, and instead invite teens to a one-on-one relationship with Jesus.

We might have to seek out the disenfranchised kids, not just the "good" kids.

We might have to love the killers, not just those who have been killed.

Prayer Leader Look through your kaleidoscope and silently name a way you have failed to let the Gospel color your ministry.

9 *L*oving God and Neighbor

Themes
- God is in love with us
- We are called to love
- Showing God's love to others
- Loving God with all your heart

Suggested Uses
- After a youth-group meeting on the theme of love for others
- During a mission trip or work camp serving others
- After a class linked to the lectionary readings for the thirtieth Sunday of Ordinary Time, Cycle A
- As part of a Valentine's Day celebration

Forms of Prayer
- Symbolic prayer
- Scripture
- Shared prayer
- Journaling
- Art
- Drama-dialogue-mime

Extra Prayer Ideas

A. Invite the teens to make and decorate two prayer cards, one with the passage "Love God with your heart, soul, and mind," and the other with the passage "Love your neighbor as yourself." Invite the teens to put one prayer card in a visible place at home. Ask them to give the other card to someone they love.

B. Before the prayer service, invite the teens to make posters or banners with the following sayings:
   - I can show my love for God by . . .
   - I can show my love for others by . . .
   Hang the posters or banners in your prayer space before you begin prayer.

C. Ask someone who knows sign language to teach the young people how to sign "Love God with your whole heart, with your whole soul, and with your whole mind." Encourage the teens to use it as a greeting between fellow youth-group leaders or classmates whenever they meet.

D. Invite the teens to write a love letter to God.

E. Give the teens a copy of resource 9–B, "Scripture Cards," to take home. Invite them to write about one of the Scripture passages in their prayer journals each day.

F. Share M&M's with the teens, along with this prayer:
   Dear God,
   Just as M&M's come in so many different colors,
     We thank you for making each one of us a truly unique, special person.
   Yet even though we are different on the outside,
     on the inside we are all connected by your great love for each one of us.
   Thank you for seeing past our often hard shells,
     to reveal what is truly sweet inside and the softness of our love for others.
   Thank you for loving us just the way we are, plain or nutty,
     and in all our tough times and colorful moods.
   Amen.

Loving God with Heart, Soul, and Mind

Materials   Gather the following items, one for each small group of no more than eight, before beginning the prayer service:

- ❑ *THE CATHOLIC YOUTH BIBLE* or another Bible
- ❑ a heart-shaped candle
- ❑ matches
- ❑ a set of Scripture hearts created from resource 9–A, "Scripture Cards"
- ❑ a sheet of red posterboard
- ❑ copies of handout 9–A, "Concluding Prayer: Loving God with Heart, Soul, and Mind," one for each teen

Preparation

- Cut eight hearts out of the red poster board.
- Make copies of resource 9–A, "Scripture Cards," one copy for each small group, and cut the Scripture quotes apart to create several sets of eight Scripture hearts.
- Set up eight stations, a good distance from one another, in your prayer or worship space, each with a Bible, a candle, matches, a poster-board heart, and a set of Scripture hearts from resource 9–A, "Scripture Cards."
- At each station, place the candle atop the red heart. Place the Scripture hearts near the candle.
- Dim the lights in the prayer space.
- Divide the large group into small groups of no more than eight.
- Ask a teen to prepare the Scripture reading:
  - ○ Matthew 22:34–40 (Love for God)
- Before the teens enter the prayer space, remind them to be reverent and quiet. Take them into the prayer space one group at a time. Tell each group to sit in a circle around its candle.

Note: This prayer service works best when it is dark outside.

Order of Prayer

Call to Prayer   **Prayer Leader:** We come together tonight to pray to a God who loves us dearly. Our theme tonight is the great commandment: Love God and others. Let us pray for the courage to love God and love others in the way Jesus taught us. Amen.

Lighting of the Prayer Candles   *[Invite one teen in each group to light their prayer candle.]*

[Invite the Scripture reader to read Matthew 22:34–40 to the large group.]

Prayer Leader: The Scriptures often call us to love God by showing love for all of God's people. Have someone in your group pick up a Scripture heart and read it to the rest of the members of your small group. Each group member will read a heart to the group.

Love for Others

Prayer Leader: Tonight we shared many ways we can show love for others. One important way we can love others is by praying for them. Each group has a red poster-board heart. You will pass those hearts around the circle. When you receive the heart, offer a brief prayer for someone in your life who needs our prayers tonight. After everyone has offered their prayers, all will respond, "Lord, hear our prayer."

Concluding Prayer

[When all the groups have concluded the prayer, distribute handout 9–A, "Concluding Prayer: Loving God with Heart, Soul, and Mind," and invite the teens to join in the concluding prayer.]

All:
God of all love,
you are love itself.
Help us follow your great commandments.

We want to love you,
with our whole heart,
with our whole soul,
and with our whole mind.

Open our eyes
to see your love in all you created,
to see your love in all we meet,
to feel your love in our toughest times.

We want to love our neighbors
as we love ourselves.

But you must understand it is tough, Lord.
It isn't even easy to love ourselves sometimes.
And even tougher to love others who put us down.

Help us realize that others see your love
reflected in each one of us.

Give us courage to be your love
to our friends, family, and all we meet.

Amen.

Prayer Leader: Go forth and be the love of God for others.

Scripture Cards

"I give you a new commandment, that you love one another. Just as I have loved you, you also should love one another." (John 13:34)

The grace of the Lord Jesus Christ, the love of God, and the communion of the Holy Spirit be with all of you. (2 Corinthians 13:13)

Praise the Lord!
O give thanks to the Lord for he is good; for his steadfast love endures forever.
(Psalm 106:1)

Clothe yourselves with compassion, kindness, humility, meekness, and patience. Bear with one another, . . . forgive each other. . . . . Above all, clothe yourselves with love. (Colossians 3:12–14)

Handout 9–A *(continued)*

And now, faith, hope, and love abide, these
three; and the greatest of these is love.
(1 Corinthians 13:13)

And that Christ may dwell in your hearts through
faith, as you are being rooted and grounded in
love. (Ephesians 3:17)

"If you love those who love you, what credit is
that to you? But I say to you that listen, Love
your enemies, do good to those who hate you."
(Luke 6:32,27)

For God so loved the world that he gave his only
Son, so that everyone who believes in him may
not perish but may have eternal life.
(John 3:16)

Concluding Prayer:
Loving God with Heart, Soul, and Mind

All:
God of all love,
you are love itself.
Help us follow your great commandments.

We want to love you,
with our whole heart,
with our whole soul,
and with our whole mind.

Open our eyes
to see your love in all you created,
to see your love in all we meet,
to feel your love in our toughest times.

We want to love our neighbors
as we love ourselves.

But you must understand it is tough, Lord.
It isn't even easy to love ourselves sometimes.
And even tougher to love others who put us down.

Help us realize that others see your love
reflected in each one of us.

Give us courage to be your love
to our friends, family, and all we meet.

Amen.

Prayer Leader   Go forth and be the love of God for others.

10

Prayer Can Be Fun!

Themes
- Making time for God
- Imagining a different way to pray
- Tasting and seeing the goodness of the Lord

Suggested Uses
- To introduce creative prayer
- To capture the imagination of teens
- To challenge the teens to approach God differently
- For evening prayer on a youth-group camping trip
- For prayer at a Catholic summer camp
- For prayer with scouts who are earning their religious medals

Forms of Prayer
- Symbolic prayer
- Shared prayer
- Journaling

Extra Prayer Ideas
A. Challenge the teens to write and share other edible prayers.
B. Place a large bowl of fruit in the center of the prayer space. Give each teen a list of the fruits of the Holy Spirit. Begin a discussion, something like this: An apple is like _____ because _____.
C. Provide materials for the teens to make and decorate small canvas drawstring prayer bags. Allow them to choose items or symbols for their bags, such as Life Savers, Band-Aids, tissues, macaroni noodles, birthday candles, small stones, Hershey's Kisses, puzzle pieces, bows, seeds, pennies, cotton balls, rubber bands, and so on. They can write prayers for each item in their prayer journals and add their own items from time to time.
D. Divide the large group into small groups of four or five. Give each small group a bag of marshmallows to share. Give them 10 minutes to list as many uses of marshmallows as they can. Share responses in a large group. Next, give the small groups 10 minutes to brainstorm as many creative ways to pray as they can. Share responses in a large group.
E. Challenge the teens to spend a week looking for faith connections in common objects and common experiences.
F. Collect the one-sentence s'more prayers that the teens create during this prayer service, and create a s'more prayer booklet. Give a copy to your parish scout troop to use for prayer.

S'more Prayer

Materials Gather the following items before beginning the prayer service:
- ❏ a s'more maker or a campfire
- ❏ marshmallows, graham crackers, and chocolate bars, enough for each teen to make two s'mores
- ❏ roasting sticks, one for each teen
- ❏ pens or pencils, one for each teen
- ❏ copies of handout 10–A, "S'more Treats and Reflection," one for each teen

Preparation
- Borrow a s'more maker or build a small campfire.
  - ○ If your group of teens is large, divide them into small groups of six to eight.

Order of Prayer

Invite the teens to make s'more treats by demonstrating the process for them:
- Break a graham cracker in half.
- Add some chocolate to one side.
- Toast a marshmallow.
- Put the toasted marshmallow on top of the chocolate.
- Add the other half of the cracker to the top.
- Enjoy!

Distribute the sticks for toasting the marshmallows. When the teens are done making their s'mores, invite them to think of a word or phrase that comes to mind when they hear the word *s'more*.

Shared Prayer in Small Groups Invite the teens, one at a time, to share their word or phase. Ask that the group not comment.

Journal Reflection Distribute a pen or pencil and a copy of handout 10–A to each teen. Ask the teens to write their word or phrase on the handout and to journal on the next two handout questions:
- How might you connect s'mores with your faith in God?
- How might you connect s'mores with your relationship with God?

Invite the teens, one at a time, to share their answers to the handout questions with their small groups.

Shared Prayer in Small Groups Ask the teens to write a one-sentence prayer inspired by the s'more (question 4 on the handout). Then invite the teens to share their prayers in their small groups. Close the prayer service by inviting the teens to make another s'more.

S'more Treats and Reflection

Making a S'more Treat
- Break a graham cracker in half.
- Add some chocolate to one side.
- Toast a marshmallow.
- Put the toasted marshmallow on top of the chocolate.
- Add the other half of the cracker to the top.
- Enjoy!

1. Write a word or phrase that comes to mind when you hear the word *s'more*.

2. How might you connect s'mores with your faith in God?

3. How might you connect s'mores with your relationship with God?

4. Write a one-sentence prayer inspired by the s'more.

11 Prayer at the Start of Something New

Themes
- Sharing your gifts
- Don't hide your gifts!
- Celebrating the gifts of youth
- Gifted to serve God and others
- Recognizing your gifts

Suggested Uses
- At the beginning of a school year or a new youth ministry or parish formation program
- As part of a parish ministry fair
- As part of World Youth Day
- At a celebration of young people

Forms of Prayer
- Music
- Petition
- Symbolic prayer
- Drama-dialogue-mime
- Scripture
- Art
- Liturgical prayer
- Storytelling
- Affirmation

Extra Prayer Ideas

A. Give each teen a sealed envelope with both a copy of "The Parable of the Talents" (Matthew 25:14–30) and a one-, two-, or five-dollar bill inside. Challenge the teens to, in a month's time, return to "the master" and share what they have done with the money given to them.

B. Ask the seniors in your parish or school to meet with the freshmen and share how they gained the courage to share their gifts and talents with the wider youth community.

C. Create a large banner that says, "You Are a Gift from God!" Hang it up in your worship space during prayer and later display it prominently in the school vestibule or youth-group meeting hall.

D. Celebrate the diversity of your parish or school community by proclaiming some of the readings or prayers from this prayer service in other languages.

The Gifts We Are

Materials Gather the following items before beginning the prayer service:
- ❑ the song "Celebrate Youth," by Steve Angrisano
- ❑ a CD of instrumental music
- ❑ two CD players
- ❑ six copies of resource 11–A, "Procession of Gifts"
- ❑ a cross
- ❑ a candle
- ❑ three or four textbooks
- ❑ a basket of food
- ❑ a wooden or cardboard model of a door signed by the teens
- ❑ two copies of THE CATHOLIC YOUTH BIBLE or another Bible
- ❑ the song "To You, O God, I Lift up My Soul," by Bob Hurd
- ❑ five copies of resource 11–B, "'The Parable of the Talents'"
- ❑ four copies of resource 11–C, "Reflection on 'The Parable of the Talents'"
- ❑ the song "Hear Our Prayer," by Tom Tomaszek
- ❑ eight copies of resource 11–D, "Prayers of Petition for Teens' Concerns"

Preparation
- If your parish or school has a youth choir, invite them to sing. Pair up a teen and an adult cantor to lead the songs.
- Ask six teens to prepare the procession on resource 11–A, "Procession of Gifts."
- Ask two teens to prepare the Scripture readings:
- 1 Corinthians 12:4–11 (There Are Many Gifts but the Same Spirit)
- Matthew 25:14–29 ("The Parable of the Talents")
- Ask five teens to prepare the mime adaptation of "The Parable of the Talents," on resource 11–B, "'The Parable of the Talents.'" One teen reads the script while the other four act out what the reader is describing.
- Ask four adults to prepare "The Parable of the Talents" reflection on resource 11–C, "Reflection on 'The Parable of the Talents.'"
- Invite eight teens to read the prayers of petition on resource 11–D, "Prayers of Petition for Teens' Concerns."
- Teach the songs "Celebrate Youth," "To You, O God, I Lift up My Soul," and "Hear Our Prayer."

Order of Prayer

Gathering Song Invite the teens and the choir to sing the first two verses of "Celebrate Youth."

Procession of Gifts

[Play some quiet instrumental music in the background during the procession.]

Reader 1: We bring up the cross of Jesus Christ, for in all we do—classes, youth group, and all our other activities—we put Jesus first.

Reader 2: We bring up a candle to represent all the spiritual activities in youth ministry, such as retreats, creative prayer, learning about the Bible, and attending Mass regularly.

Reader 3: We bring up some textbooks to represent the many ways we learn in youth ministry, especially through our classes.

Reader 4: We bring up a basket of food to represent all the outreach projects at *[name of parish or school]*, such as *[list some outreach projects]* and many others.

Reader 5: We bring up a CD player to represent all the social activities in our youth groups, such as *[list some activities]*.

Reader 6: We bring up a door signed by many of our teens to represent that the door is always open, that all teens are welcome at *[name of parish or school]*.

Prayer Leader: We gather together tonight in the name of the Father, and of the Son, and of the Holy Spirit.

All: Amen.

Prayer Leader: We gather as teens, parents, teachers, and friends. We ask God's blessings on the start of a new year of youth ministry at *[name of parish or school]*. We ask God to help us recognize our gifts and talents and encourage others to share their gifts and talents. We ask all this through Christ, our Lord.

All: Amen.

[Invite the teens and the choir to sing two more verses of "Celebrate Youth."]

First Reading

Invite the first Scripture reader to read 1 Corinthians 12:4–11.

Responsorial Psalm

Invite the teens and the choir to sing "To You, O God, I Lift up My Soul."

Second Reading and Dramatization

Invite the second Scripture reader to read Matthew 25:14–29.

Invite the five teens to come forward and present the Gospel using the mime script on resource 11–B, "'The Parable of the Talents.'"

Reflection

Invite the four adults to come forward and present the reflection on resource 11–C, "Reflection on 'The Parable of the Talents.'"

Prayers of Petition

Cantor: The sung response is: "Hear our prayer. Hear our prayer. Hear our prayer, Lord, hear our prayer. Hear our prayer."

[The sung response is from the song "Hear Our Prayer."]

All respond.

Reader 1: Hear our prayer, Lord, as we pray for all the teens in our parish community. Give them courage to use their gifts and talents to serve God and others.

Cantor and all respond.

Reader 2: Hear our prayer, Lord, as we pray for the catechists of our young people. Inspire them to use their gifts to share your Gospel with enthusiasm. Hear our prayer.

Cantor and all respond.

Reader 3: Hear our prayer, Lord, as we pray for the parents of all our teens. Help them share their gifts of faith, hope, and love with their children.

Cantor and all respond.

Reader 4: Hear our prayer, Lord, as we pray for world, national, and Church leaders. Teach them to be advocates for our teens entrusted to their protection.

Cantor and all respond.

Reader 5: Hear our prayer, Lord, as we pray for all teens that are homeless, hungry, and in danger. Give them shelter, food, and a safe haven this night and always.

Cantor and all respond.

Reader 6: Hear our prayer, Lord, as we pray for members of our families and parish community that are sick. Help them mend, recover, and regain physical and emotional health.

Cantor and all respond.

Reader 7: Hear our prayer, Lord, as we pray for members of our families and parish community that have died. Grant them eternal rest at your side and comfort all those who grieve their loss.

Cantor and all respond.

Reader 8: Hear our prayer, Lord, for the intentions we mention in the silence of our hearts. *[Pause.]* Guide us and comfort us, challenge us and celebrate with us, teach us and forgive us. Be with us always.

Cantor and all respond.

The Lord's Prayer   Lead the group in saying the Lord's Prayer.

Closing Blessing   **Prayer Leader:**
May God the Father bless you and keep you,
May the light of Christ shine upon you,
May the Holy Spirit bring you peace.
Amen.

Sending-Forth Song   Invite the teens and the choir to sing "Celebrate Youth."

Procession of Gifts

Reader 1   We bring up the cross of Jesus Christ, for in all we do—classes, youth group, and all our other activities—we put Jesus first.

Reader 2   We bring up a candle to represent all the spiritual activities in youth ministry, such as retreats, creative prayer, learning about the Bible, and attending Mass regularly.

Reader 3   We bring up some textbooks to represent the many ways we learn in youth ministry, especially through our classes.

Reader 4   We bring up a basket of food to represent all the outreach projects at *[name of parish or school]*, such as *[list some outreach projects]* and many others.

Reader 5   We bring up a CD player to represent all the social activities in our youth groups, such as *[list some activities]*.

Reader 6   We bring up a door signed by many of our teens to represent that the door is always open, that all teens are welcome at *[name of parish or school]*.

Prayer Leader   We gather together tonight in the name of the Father, and of the Son, and of the Holy Spirit.

All   Amen.

Prayer Leader   We gather as teens, parents, teachers, and friends. We ask God's blessings on the start of a new year of youth ministry at *[name of parish or school]*. We ask God to help us recognize our gifts and talents and encourage others to share their gifts and talents. We ask all this through Christ, Our Lord.

All   Amen.

"The Parable of the Talents"

A man was packing his bags, about to leave home on a trip.

He called to his servants to put them in charge of his property.

He gave to each one according to his ability.

To one he gave five thousand dollars.
To another two thousand dollars.
And to the other one thousand dollars.

Then he left on his trip.

The servant who had received five thousand dollars wasted no time before scattering seed on his master's land.

And in due time, plentiful crops grew and grew on the land.

When the crops were ready, he gathered them into the barn, sold them at market, and earned another five thousand dollars.

The servant who had received two thousand dollars did not know how to farm . . . but he knew how to juggle, and how to play the flute.

So he took his master's money and invested it in a circus:

He juggled, walked the tightrope,

and thrilled the crowds with his acrobatics.

The crowds enjoyed the show so much that he earned another two thousand dollars.

But the servant who had received one thousand dollars was frightened, and guarded his master's money very carefully for fear someone would steal it.

So he dug a hole, and buried the money in the ground.

After a long time, the master came back and called to his servants.

The first servant came in and said:
"Sir, you gave me five thousand dollars.
I planted seed on your land and harvested crops.

Here is the five thousand dollars I have earned."

The master said:

"Well done, good and faithful servant,
I will put you in charge of all of my land.
Come, share my happiness."

The second servant came in and said:
"Sir, you gave me two thousand dollars.
I opened a circus, and by juggling,

and doing somersaults,

I have earned a second two thousand dollars."

The master said:
"Well done, good and faithful servant,
I will put you in charge of many circuses.
Come, share my happiness."

The third servant came in and said:
"Sir, you reap harvests where you do not plant,
gather crops where you did not scatter seed:

I was afraid of losing your money.
So I took the thousand dollars and buried it in the ground.

Here is what belongs to you."

"You bad and lazy servant," said the master.

"You should have at least put my money in the bank where it could gain interest while I was gone.

Take the money from him,

and give it to those who have done well.

For to every one who has,
even more will be given.

But to the one who has nothing,
even the little he has will be taken away from him."

(Adapted from *Growing with Jesus: Sixteen Half-day, Full-day, and Overnight Retreats That Help Children Celebrate and Share the Light of Christ,* by Maryann Hakowski [Notre Dame, IN: Ave Maria Press, 1993], pages 238–239. Copyright © 1993 by Ave Maria Press, Notre Dame, IN 46556. Used with permission.)

Reflection on "The Parable of the Talents"

Reader 1   The first servant . . . This person is the enthusiastic one, ready to share his or her gifts and talents. He or she is first to respond when a question is asked. He or she comes early to set up the room. He or she makes the flyer for the youth-group meeting and the poster for the bowling trip. He or she might play soccer or sing in the choir. He or she is already trying to use his or her gifts to serve God and others. We need to encourage and support this person. He or she needs to welcome others and challenge others to share their gifts. We need to celebrate others and all they have to offer. And get them involved in building the Reign of God.

Reader 2   The second servant . . . This person has a really good heart and wants to do well but hasn't quite found her or his niche yet. But when she or he does, you will be surprised by her or his enthusiasm and creativity. She or he may not come the first time you invite her or him, but she or he will come the next time. She or he may not talk until the third class, but when she or he does, she or he will have something to say. One day she or he will surprise you and herself or himself by coming up with the best idea for a youth-group activity, by offering the most powerful prayer in class, by giving a moving witness talk on retreat. We need to help her or him find her or his gifts and give her or him the freedom to be herself or himself. We need to pray for and with her or him, and someday she or he may be leading prayer.

Reader 3   The third servant . . . This person has buried his or her gifts in the ground. Sometimes it is others who have buried them with their words and actions. He or she is pretty down on himself or herself. He or she has heard too many people say, "You can't do anything," "You're just a teenager," and "Why can't you get it right?" He or she doesn't believe he or she has anything to offer. He or she doesn't want to try new things for fear of failing. He or she doesn't want to meet new people, for fear of getting laughed at. He or she doesn't want to come to class or to youth group and is not here tonight. I pray for him or her with my whole heart. We must believe in and encourage him or her without pushing too hard. We need to convince him or her that he or she has gifts, then help him or her use those gifts. He or she needs so much for us to tell him or her that God loves him or her so very much. And God shows God's love for him or her through us.

Reader 4   The Master (AKA God) . . . The master gives gifts to all servants—all servants—according to their ability. That means we all have gifts. God has given us all gifts. God celebrates with those who use their gifts wisely. And gives us a kick in the tail when we need to get our act together. I believe in a God of second chances. I hope the servant got it right the next time, and hopefully the first two servants showed her or him the ropes.

Prayers of Petition for Teens' Concerns

Cantor   The sung response is: "Hear our prayer. Hear our prayer. Hear our prayer, Lord, hear our prayer. Hear our prayer."

[The sung response is from the song "Hear Our Prayer."]

All respond.

Reader 1   Hear our prayer, Lord, as we pray for all the teens in our parish community. Give them courage to use their gifts and talents to serve God and others.

Cantor and all respond.

Reader 2   Hear our prayer, Lord, as we pray for the catechists of our young people. Inspire them to use their gifts to share your Gospel with enthusiasm. Hear our prayer.

Cantor and all respond.

Reader 3   Hear our prayer, Lord, as we pray for the parents of all our teens. Help them share their gifts of faith, hope, and love with their children.

Cantor and all respond.

Reader 4   Hear our prayer, Lord, as we pray for world, national, and church leaders. Teach them to be advocates for our teens entrusted to their protection.

Cantor and all respond.

Reader 5   Hear our prayer, Lord, as we pray for all teens that are homeless, hungry, and in danger. Give them shelter, food, and a safe haven this night and always.

Cantor and all respond.

Reader 6   Hear our prayer, Lord, as we pray for members of our families and parish community that are sick. Help them mend, recover, and regain physical and emotional health.

Cantor and all respond.

Reader 7   Hear our prayer, Lord, as we pray for members of our families and parish community that have died. Grant them eternal rest at your side and comfort all those who grieve their loss.

Cantor and all respond.

Reader 8   Hear our prayer, Lord, for the intentions we mention in the silence of our hearts.

[Pause.]

Guide us and comfort us, challenge us and celebrate with us, teach us and forgive us. Be with us always.

Cantor and all respond.

12 $\mathcal{W}$e Are the Body of Christ

Themes
- We are the Body of Christ
- One body, many parts
- Sharing our story
- Sticking together
- Unity is strength

Suggested Uses
- To build community
- To address conflict within a group
- As part of a parish family program
- To encourage or celebrate outreach in a group
- To celebrate and recognize how all gifts are needed
- To help explain that the Church is living, giving people

Forms of Prayer
- Music
- Scripture
- Storytelling
- Shared prayer
- Symbolic prayer
- Journaling

Extra Prayer Ideas
A. Use the topic "The Body of Christ Is a Real Presence" for a follow-up discussion.
B. Ask the teens, in small groups, to develop stories about what would happen if Jesus were part of our daily life. For example, different groups could tell what would happen if Jesus were to come to dinner; if Jesus were to come to school; or if he were part of our youth group, team, or other activity. After the teens share the stories, ask them if they think Jesus's presence would change us. Allow them to discuss.
C. Invite the teens to find themselves, their families, and God in the story, "A Bundle of Sticks," on resource 12–A. Follow the story with quiet journal time.
D. Send part of this prayer service, or the story on resource 12–A, "A Bundle of Sticks," home with the teens to discuss with their families.

Let's Stick Together

Materials

Gather the following items before beginning the prayer service:

☐ the song "The Song of the Body of Christ," by No Ke Ano' Ah and David Haas)

☐ two copies of THE CATHOLIC YOUTH BIBLE or another Bible

☐ one copy of resource 12–A, "'A Bundle of Sticks'"

☐ sticks, one for each teen

☐ a length of colorful yarn, long enough to tie all the sticks together when they are piled together

Preparation

- Ask two teens to prepare the Scripture readings:
  ○ 1 Corinthians 12:12–26 (One Body with Many Members)
  ○ Ephesians 4:1–6 (Unity in the Body of Christ)
- Teach the song "The Song of the Body of Christ."
- Prepare some examples to share when introducing "The Body Reaches Out" part of the prayer. Examples might include the following:
  ○ taking time to listen to others
  ○ accepting someone who is different
  ○ doing a random act of kindness
  ○ calling someone who is sick
- Prepare some examples to share when introducing "The Body Is Divided" part of the prayer. Examples might include the following:
  ○ jealousy of others' possessions
  ○ competition rather than cooperation
  ○ thoughtlessness or meanness
  ○ speaking before thinking
- Ask a teen to prepare the story on resource 12–A, "'A Bundle of Sticks.'"
- Invite an adult youth leader to give a short reflection on the theme "Let's Stick with One Another."
- Ask a teen to prepare the mantra.

Order of Prayer

Call to Prayer

Gather the teens in a large circle. Invite the group to sing the refrain and verse one of "The Song of the Body of Christ." As they sing, place a stick at the feet of each teen.

First Reading

Invite the first Scripture reader to read 1 Corinthians 12:12–26.

Invite the group to sing the refrain and verse two of "The Song of the Body of Christ."

The Body Reaches Out	Direct the teens, one at a time, to take the hand of another and complete this sentence: The Body reaches out by . . .
	Ask the group to sing the refrain and verse three of "The Song of the Body of Christ."
The Body Is Divided	Tell the teens, one at a time, to break the chain of hands and complete this sentence: The Body is divided by . . .
	Invite the group to sing the refrain and verse four of "The Song of the Body of Christ."
Storytelling	Direct the story reader to read the story by Bill Gordh on resource 12–A, "'A Bundle of Sticks.'"
	Ask the teens to place their sticks in a pile in the center of the prayer space, half of them lengthwise and half of them crosswise to create a cross. Wrap the sticks together with some colorful yarn. Leave the cross in the center of the prayer space and continue with the prayer service.
	Direct the group to sing the refrain and verse five of "The Song of the Body of Christ."
Reflection on the Theme "Let's Stick with One Another"	*[Invite the adult youth leader to present his or her reflection on the theme "Let's Stick with One Another."]*
	Mantra Reader: I am the Body of Christ. We are the Body of Christ.
	[Invite each person to join in until everyone is participating and the mantra is very loud.]
Second Reading	Invite the second Scripture reader to read Ephesians 4:1–6.
	Invite the group to sing the refrain of "The Song of the Body of Christ."

"A Bundle of Sticks"

A Kenyan Fable by Bill Gordh

Once there was a family with many children: thirteen in all, seven sisters and six brothers. There was always plenty of excitement around their house. Most of the time the children played and worked well together. They helped their mama and papa with jobs around their home, such as making baskets, gathering food, and fetching water for washing clothes and cooking. Also, each child was proud to tend his or her own garden. When not working, the children played. Mostly they had fun, but sometimes they would argue. Sometimes they did not like to share. Sometimes they said mean things and hurt one another's feelings, and it seemed to Papa that lately the only thing his children did was argue.

One morning Papa was in his garden when he heard the children arguing once again. Papa listened. He heard some mean name-calling, and then two of his children crying, and then more mean words and more arguing, and on and on. Papa hurried from the garden, trying to think about what he should do. He got an idea.

Papa called to his children to come to him. He wiped away tears and gave out hugs. Everyone finally calmed down. Then he began his plan. He asked his children to stand in a big circle. Next he said, "My circle of children, go quietly into the woods. Each of you find one stick and bring it back into the circle." The children wondered what their papa was planning as they ran off into the woods.

[Stop reading here and instruct the group to go outside, pick up a stick, and return quickly to the prayer space.]

One by one the children came back into the circle, each with a stick in his or her hand. Now Papa walked inside the circle, all the way around, looking at each child. Then he stopped in front of one of his daughters. He asked her to try and break her stick. She looked at her papa. He said again, "Go on, try to break your stick." She did. Snap! She smiled. He moved to the next child. "Try to break your stick," he said to his son. His son looked at him and . . . snap! Papa moved around the circle, repeating to each child, "Try to break your stick." Snap! Snap! Snap! Snap! Thirteen sticks snapped, and now there were thirteen confused children standing in a circle, each with two sticks in hand.

Papa collected the sticks and put them together in a bundle, which he handed to one of his children. "Try to break the sticks," he said. "Go on, try to break the sticks." She tried. No snap. She tried some more. The sticks would not break. Papa took the bundle and handed it to the next child. "Try to break the sticks," he said. The boy tried as hard as he could, but they would not break. Papa went around the circle, handing the bundle again to each of his children and repeating, "Try to break the sticks." The sticks would not break. Then he asked his children to sit down and hold hands. They all sat down together in a circle and held hands. Papa placed the bundle of sticks in the center, looked around his circle of children, and asked, "How can our family be strong?"

"Together!" said all the children at once. "Together!"

(Adapted from the story "A Bundle of Sticks," from *Sesame Street Parents Magazine*, December 1998/January 1999 issue)

13

The Waters of Baptism

Themes
- God moves in the water
- We are called by Baptism
- Thirsting for God
- Baptized with Jesus
- Come to the water!

Suggested Uses
- At the beginning of a retreat
- As part of a youth-group meeting or class on the sacraments
- As part of a Scripture study group

Forms of Prayer
- Music
- Scripture
- Litany
- Symbolic prayer
- Sacramental prayer
- Petition
- Storytelling

Extra Prayer Ideas
- A. Challenge the teens to find and reflect on some of the Scripture text found in the "Litany of the Waters." How does water play a key role in each passage? How can we connect this Scripture text to our own lives?
- B. Invite your parish music minister to teach some other African-American spirituals.
- C. Invite the teens to pray for the newly baptized in your parish.
- D. Invite someone who has been recently baptized into the Catholic faith to share his or her journey to Baptism and his or her experience of being baptized.

We Are Thirsty, Lord

Materials   Gather the following items before beginning the prayer service:
- ❑ the song "Come to the Water," by John Foley
- ❑ THE CATHOLIC YOUTH BIBLE or another Bible
- ❑ one copy of resource 13–A, "Litany of the Waters"
- ❑ a baptismal font or large, clear bowl of holy water
- ❑ the song "Wade in the Water," by M. D. Ridge

Preparation
- Invite someone to prepare, teach, and lead "Come to the Water" and "Wade in the Water."
- Ask a teen to prepare the Scripture reading:
  - Matthew 3:13–17 (The Baptism of Jesus)
- Ask an adult youth leader or older teen to prepare the reflection on living out our Baptism.
- Ask another teen prepare the litany.
- Reserve the worship space and font area of your church.

Order of Prayer

Call to Prayer   **Prayer Leader:** God of Water, God of life, renew and refresh us this day. Help us answer our baptismal call to serve you and others in our everyday lives.

Opening Song   Invite the group to sing "Come to the Water."

Reading   Invite the Scripture reader to read Matthew 3:13–17.

Reflection   Invite the adult youth leader or older teen to come forward and present his or her reflection on the theme "We are called to live out our Baptism throughout our entire lives."

Litany of the Waters   **Litany Leader:** We are thirsty, Lord. Our response is, "Come, renew us."

[Pause for all to respond after each line of the litany.]

Gift of the creator . . .
River of salvation . . .
Water that tossed the ark of Noah . . .
Water that withdrew to a new promise . . .
Sea that parted for the Chosen People . . .
Water that flowed from the desert rock . . .

Water that baptizes Jesus at the hand of John . . .
Water that begins the ministry of Jesus . . .
Water shared at the well of a stranger . . .
Water changed miraculously into wine . . .
Water Jesus calmed on a turbulent sea . . .
Water he walked on to inspire great faith . . .
Living water promised to bring eternal life . . .
Water he gently poured on the feet of his disciples . . .
Water of the Father, Son and Holy Spirit . . .

Tears Jesus cried for Lazarus . . .
Tears of compassion for all who suffer . . .
Tears he wept for the city of Jerusalem . . .
Tears of the women on the road to Calvary . . .

Water and blood poured from Jesus's side on the cross . . .

Water of Baptism that buries us with Christ . . .
Water of Baptism that raises us to new life . . .

Water that washes away our sins . . .
Water that brings us forgiveness and hope . . .
Water drawn from the depth of our wells . . .
Water shared at the well with friends . . .
Water to renew our dry lands . . .
Water to fill our empty jars . . .
Water to quench our spiritual thirst . . .

Invitation to Come to the Water   Invite the teens to come forward to the font to bless themselves and renew their commitment to live out their baptismal call.

Concluding Song   Invite the group to sing "Wade in the Water."

Litany of the Waters

Litany Leader   We are thirsty, Lord. Our response is, "Come, renew us."

[Pause for all to respond after each line of the litany.]

Gift of the creator . . .
River of salvation . . .
Water that tossed the ark of Noah . . .
Water that withdrew to a new promise . . .
Sea that parted for the Chosen People . . .
Water that flowed from the desert rock . . .

Water that baptizes Jesus at the hand of John . . .
Water that begins the ministry of Jesus . . .
Water shared at the well of a stranger . . .
Water changed miraculously into wine . . .
Water Jesus calmed on a turbulent sea . . .
Water he walked on to inspire great faith . . .
Living water promised to bring eternal life . . .
Water he gently poured on the feet of his disciples . . .
Water of the Father, Son, and Holy Spirit . . .

Tears Jesus cried for Lazarus . . .
Tears of compassion for all who suffer . . .
Tears he wept for the city of Jerusalem . . .
Tears of the women on the road to Calvary . . .

Water and blood poured from Jesus's side on the cross . . .

Water of Baptism that buries us with Christ . . .
Water of Baptism that raises us to new life . . .

Water that washes away our sins . . .
Water that brings us forgiveness and hope . . .
Water drawn from the depth of our wells . . .
Water shared at the well with friends . . .
Water to renew our dry lands . . .
Water to fill our empty jars . . .
Water to quench our spiritual thirst . . .

14 Prayer for Confirmation Preparation

Themes
- Gifts of the Spirit
- Preparing for Confirmation
- Offering guidance
- Confirming faith
- Spirit as gift from Jesus

Suggested Uses
- At the first meeting of the Confirmation candidates, parents, and sponsors

Forms of Prayer
- Scripture
- Storytelling
- Litany
- Symbolic prayer
- Music
- Reflection
- Art
- Journaling
- Petition
- Shared prayer

Extra Prayer Ideas

A. Invite the teens to write a prayer for the sponsors. Ask the sponsors to write a prayer for the candidates. Weave them into each of your meetings or create a small book of prayers.

B. Each time you gather, use a different gift of the Holy Spirit for shared Prayers of the Faithful. You may also use the fruits of the Spirit (see Galatians 5:22–23).

C. Invite the teens to choose songs that inspire or guide them on their faith journey. Play one song per week with a 3-minute reflection on the faith theme. Start a Confirmation song list and pass it on to the next class.

D. Ask the teens who were confirmed the year prior to serve as prayer partners for the new candidates or to assist as prayer and retreat leaders.

E. Start a Confirmation prayer intention book decorated with symbols of Confirmation. The sponsors, candidates, other teens, teachers, and parents can write in it. Use prayers during class each week.

Gifts of the Spirit

Materials   Gather the following items before beginning the prayer service:
- ❑ a copy of the CD *We Are Fire: Companion Songs for "The Catholic Youth Bible®"* (Comet Records, 1999)
- ❑ a CD player
- ❑ copies of handout 14–A, "Gifts of the Spirit," one for each teen
- ❑ THE CATHOLIC YOUTH BIBLE or another Bible
- ❑ one copy of resource 14–A, "'The Inner Lion'"
- ❑ a red pillar candle (the Confirmation candle)
- ❑ matches

Preparation
- • Cue the song "You are the Way" on the *We Are Fire!* CD.
- • Ask a teen to prepare the Scripture reading:
  - ○ John 14:15–17,25–26 (Jesus Promises to Send the Holy Spirit)
- • Ask a parent to prepare the story on resource 14–A, "'The Inner Lion.'"
- • Ask a sponsor to light the Confirmation candle at the appropriate time.

Order of Prayer

Opening Song   Play the song "You are the Way."

Prayer for Wisdom and Knowledge   *[Distribute a copy of handout 14–A, "Gifts of the Spirit," to each participant. Direct them to "Prayer for Wisdom and Knowledge" on the handout.]*

Candidates: Spirit, we pray for the gift of knowledge so we can learn as much as we can about our faith.

Parents: We pray for knowledge and wisdom, to make the right decisions in raising our youth.

Sponsors: We pray for wisdom, to guide our youth on their faith journey.

Reading   Invite the Scripture reader to read John 14:15–17,25–26.

Prayer for Courage   *[Direct the participants to "Prayer for Courage" on handout 14–A, "Gifts of the Spirit."]*

Candidates: Spirit, we pray for the courage to be ourselves in a world where everyone wants us to be someone else.

Parents: We pray for the courage to raise our young people as Catholics in an increasingly anti-Christian world.

Sponsors: We pray for the courage to live what we believe and be an example to the Confirmation candidates.

Story

Direct the story reader to read the story and give the reflection on resource 14–A, "'The Inner Lion.'"

Prayer for Counsel and Understanding

[Direct the participants to "Prayer for Counsel and Understanding" on handout 14–A, "Gifts of the Spirit."]

Candidates: Spirit, we pray for the gift of understanding, so we can understand your word and be more understanding toward others.

Parents: We pray that our young people will be able to reach out to us when they struggle with problems.

Sponsors: We pray for the gift of counsel so we can find the right words to comfort young people who struggle in life.

Lighting of the Confirmation Candle

Invite the sponsor to light the Confirmation candle.

Direct the participants to offer silent prayers for the Confirmation candidates.

Prayer for Reverence, Wonder, and Awe

[Direct the participants to "Prayer for Reverence, Wonder, and Awe" on handout 14–A, "Gifts of the Spirit."]

Candidates: We pray for the gift of reverence, to be able to treat ourselves and others with respect.

Parents: We pray that the gift of wonder and awe will fill us with thanksgiving for the gift of our families.

Sponsors: We pray to be able to share a sense of reverence in prayer for and with our young people.

[Direct the participants to "Concluding Prayer" on handout 14–A, "Gifts of the Spirit."]

Concluding   **All:**
God of light, from whom all good gifts come,
send your Spirit into our lives
with the power of a mighty wind,
and with the flame of your wisdom,
open the horizons of our minds.

Give us the grace to sing your praise
in words beyond the power of speech,
for without your Spirit,
we could never raise our voice in words of peace
or announce the truth that Jesus is Lord,
who lives and reigns with you and the Holy Spirit,
one God, for ever and ever.

Amen.

Gifts of the Spirit

Prayer for Wisdom and Knowledge

Candidates: Spirit, we pray for the gift of knowledge so we can learn as much as we can about our faith.

Parents: We pray for knowledge and wisdom, to make the right decisions in raising our youth.

Sponsors: We pray for wisdom, to guide our youth on their faith journey.

Prayer for Courage

Candidates: Spirit, we pray for the courage to be ourselves in a world where everyone wants us to be someone else.

Parents: We pray for the courage to raise our young people as Catholics in an increasingly anti-Christian world.

Sponsors: We pray for the courage to live what we believe and be an example to the Confirmation candidates.

Prayer for Counsel and Understanding

Candidates: Spirit, we pray for the gift of understanding, so we can understand your word and be more understanding toward others.

Parents: We pray that our young people will be able to reach out to us when they struggle with problems.

Sponsors: We pray for the gift of counsel so we can find the right words to comfort young people who struggle in life.

Prayer for Reverence, Wonder, and Awe

Candidates: We pray for the gift of reverence, to be able to treat ourselves and others with respect.

Parents: We pray that the gift of wonder and awe will fill us with thanksgiving for the gift of our families.

Sponsors: We pray to be able to share a sense of reverence in prayer for and with our young people.

Concluding Prayer   **All:**
God of light, from whom all good gifts come,
send your Spirit into our lives
with the power of a mighty wind,
and with the flame of your wisdom,
open the horizons of our minds.

Give us the grace to sing your praise
in words beyond the power of speech,
for without your Spirit,
we could never raise our voice in words of peace
or announce the truth that Jesus is Lord,
who lives and reigns with you and the Holy Spirit,
one God, for ever and ever.

Amen.

"The Inner Lion"

This story takes place in the workshop of a great and famous sculptor who lived in Italy a long time ago.

Once, as the sculptor was beginning to work on a new block of marble, he noticed a young boy standing in the doorway of his shop. The boy didn't say anything. He just stood watching the great man chisel away at the block.

The boy came often to the sculptor's shop. He watched the chunks of marble fall away one by one—first large chunks, then finer and finer pieces—until he could see a form emerging from the marble.

One day the boy arrived at the shop to find that the block of marble had been transformed into a magnificent lion, poised and powerful and larger than life. For a long time, the boy stood in amazement just looking at the lion. Finally, he turned to the sculptor and said, "Hey, mister, how did you know there was a lion inside that marble?"

(Adapted from *Existential Metapsychiatry*, by Thomas Hora [New York: Seabury Press, 1977], pages 20–21. Copyright © 1977 by Seabury Press.)

Reflection In a way, the boy was right. There was a lion inside the marble. In a way, that is what our Confirmation program is all about. In each person, in each Confirmation candidate, there is an inner lion, an inner faith. The aim of this program is to help bring that faith to the surface, to strengthen it and deepen it and share it with others. There are some problems and doubts to chisel away. There are many questions to answer along the way. But that inner faith is already present in you. So, then, on Confirmation day, you will Confirm your faith.

15 Getting More Out of Mass

Themes
- Opening yourself up to God
- Using your five senses in prayer
- Getting more out of Mass

Suggested Uses
- To encourage regular, active attendance and participation at Mass
- As part of a class on the Mass
- As a follow-up to a discussion on the importance of creativity and prayer

Forms of Prayer
- Reflection
- Journaling
- Shared prayer
- Liturgical prayer
- Symbolic prayer

Extra Prayer Ideas

A. Compare attending a live sporting event with watching the same event on TV, alone. Compare attending Mass with friends and family to praying all alone. Ask, "What happens when you arrive late for a movie, or when you have to leave the movie before it ends?" Ask, "How do you experience Mass differently when you come early and stay late?"

B. After making popcorn, invite the teens to write a popcorn prayer about experiencing God. Seal the popcorn in clear plastic bags tied with ribbon or yarn, and direct teens to attach their popcorn prayer. Teens can give the bag of popcorn as a gift.

C. Use the following questions as take-home reflection questions for responding to in a prayer journal:
- How is popcorn transformed when placed in a popcorn popper?
- How are we transformed when we attend Mass on Sunday?

D. Invite small groups to plan prayer services based on the theme "Blessing the Bread" to share with the larger group. The following questions will help get the teens thinking about the theme:
- What Scripture passages talk about breaking bread, the heavenly feast, or sharing meals?
- What song would work with the passage?
- What symbol would you like to use?
- Do you know any "grace before meal" prayers that you could adapt to fit the theme, or would you like to create your own blessing?

Let Our Prayers Rise Like Popcorn

Materials

Gather the following items before beginning the prayer service:

❑ the song "Open My Eyes," by Jesse Manibusan

❑ an unpopped bag of microwave popcorn

❑ a popcorn popper with a clear lid

❑ unpopped popcorn and vegetable oil, enough so that everyone in the group will get some popcorn to eat

❑ melted butter and salt, if desired

❑ napkins, one for each teen

Preparation

• Set the popcorn popper where all the teens can see it clearly. If you have a very large group, you may need more than one popper.

• Prepare the popcorn popper with the appropriate ingredients.

• Teach the song "Open My Eyes."

Order of Prayer

Opening Song

Invite the teens to sing "Open My Eyes."

Call to Prayer

Prayer Leader: Can anyone tell me what this is? *[Hold up the unopened bag of microwave popcorn.]* How do you make popcorn this way? *[Allow the teens to answer.]* When you make popcorn in the microwave, you can hear it and smell it while it is popping, but you can't see it popping. You can't tell if it is done unless you open the bag. And you better do that carefully, or you might get burned. Have you ever made popcorn in a popcorn popper? We're going to make popcorn together tonight. Pay close attention. There will be a quiz.

[Make popcorn in the popcorn popper. Distribute the napkins, and invite everyone to try some of the popcorn when it is done.]

Reflection Questions on Sharing Popcorn

Ask the teens the following questions. Invite them to first share their answers in pairs and then share in a large group around the popper.

• During this demonstration, what did you see?

• What did you hear?

• What did you smell?

• What did you taste?

• What did you touch?

Large-Group Questions on Sharing Popcorn

Ask the teens the following questions, and then summarize the answers when the group is done discussing:
- What is the difference between making microwave popcorn and making popcorn in a popper?
- What can making popcorn teach us about prayer?

Reflection on Liturgy

[Ask the teens to move into your worship space. Invite them to sit up front.]

Prayer Leader: Think about the last time you attended Mass. Were you really there, or was your mind wandering elsewhere? Were you a spectator or a participant? Were you really aware of all that was going on around you?

Reflection Questions on Attending Mass

Ask the teens the following questions. Invite them to first share their answers in pairs and then share in a large group around the popper.
- The last time you attended Mass, what did you see?
- What did you hear?
- What did you smell?
- What did you taste?
- What did you touch?

Large-Group Questions on Attending Mass

Ask the teens the following questions, and then summarize the answers when the group is done discussing:
- What has this discussion taught you about the way you approach liturgy?
- Why do we sometimes take Mass for granted?
- How can popping popcorn teach us to really experience the Mass?

Concluding Song

Invite the teens to sing "Open My Eyes."

16 *A* Sacramental Prayer

Themes
- Baptism
- Reconciliation
- The Eucharist
- Confirmation
- Matrimony
- Holy Orders
- Anointing of the Sick

Suggested Uses
- At a youth-group meeting on Catholic identity
- As a prayer for a retreat on the sacraments

Forms of Prayer
- Symbolic prayer
- Petition
- Sacramental prayer
- Art
- Journaling
- Liturgical prayer
- Storytelling

Extra Prayer Ideas
A. Invite the teens to pray, by name if possible, for those receiving sacraments. Perhaps they can make prayer cards as an outreach project.
B. Invite someone who has just received one of the sacraments to give a witness talk about his or her decision and experience.
C. Recruit parishioners as prayer partners for the teens approaching Confirmation.
D. Invite the teens to read the Prayer of the Faithful at liturgy on Sunday.
E. Invite the teens and their families to the Easter Vigil to celebrate with those being baptized, those being confirmed, and those receiving first Eucharist.
F. Use each of the prayer sections at different classes, and add a journaling activity.

Signs and Wonders

Materials Gather the following items before beginning the prayer service:
- ☐ a baptismal candle
- ☐ chrism
- ☐ a white garment
- ☐ seven copies of THE CATHOLIC YOUTH BIBLE or another Bible
- ☐ a candle
- ☐ a purple stole
- ☐ a loaf of bread
- ☐ a chalice
- ☐ a paten
- ☐ a red cloth
- ☐ a kneeler for two
- ☐ plain rings to simulate wedding rings
- ☐ a set of unity candles
- ☐ a stole
- ☐ oil of the sick
- ☐ a pyx
- ☐ the song "Who Calls You by Name?" by David Haas

Preparation
- Place symbols at each of the seven sites, as indicated in the order of prayer.
- Ask two teens to lead the prayer at each session.
- Ask seven teens to read the Scripture passages:
  - Mark 1:9–11 (Jesus is Baptized by John)
  - Matthew 18:21–22 (How Often Should I Forgive?)
  - Mark 14:22–25 (The Last Supper)
  - Acts 2:1–4 (Pentecost)
  - John 2:1–11 (The Wedding at Cana)
  - Matthew 9:35–38 (The Harvest is Great, the Laborers Few)
  - Luke 18:35–43 (Jesus Heals a Blind Beggar Near Jericho)
- Teach the teens the prayer response and indicate by gesture when they are to respond during the service.
- Ask a teen or adult to take the part of the cantor, and to teach the teens the refrain of "Who Calls You by Name?"

Order of Prayer

Baptism   *[Lead the group to the baptismal font near the Easter candle, where you have placed water in the font, a baptismal candle, chrism, and a white garment.]*

[Invite the group to sing the refrain of "Who Calls You by Name?"]

Teen Prayer Leader 1: Our response is, "Fill us with your grace."

All: Fill us with your grace.

Teen Prayer Leader 1: Let us pray for all children who are baptized into our parish community that they and their parents continue to grow in faith.

All: Fill us with your grace.

Teen Prayer Leader 2: Let us pray for adults who take a leap of faith into our font and become part of our faith through the sacrament of Baptism.

All: Fill us with your grace.

First Reading   Invite the Scripture reader to read Mark 1:9–11.

[Lead the group to the Reconciliation room or confessional, where you have placed a candle and purple stole.]

[Invite the group to sing the refrain of "Who Calls You by Name?"]

Teen Prayer Leader 1: Let us pray for the children and teens about to receive the sacrament of Reconciliation for the first time, that they may experience the joy of God's great gift of forgiveness.

All: Fill us with your grace.

Teen Prayer Leader 2: Let us pray for all those who are separated by sin from God and others, that they may find the courage to receive the sacrament of Reconciliation.

All: Fill us with your grace.

Second Reading   Invite the Scripture reader to read Matthew 18:21–22.

The Eucharist   *[Lead the group to the altar, where you have placed a loaf of bread, a chalice, and a paten.]*

[Invite the group to sing the refrain of "Who Calls You by Name?"]

Teen Prayer Leader 1: Let us pray for all who will receive first Eucharist this year, that they may grow daily in the love of Christ.

All: Fill us with your grace.

Teen Prayer Leader 2: Let us pray for our parish community, that we may come often to the table of the Lord to be nourished in body and soul.

All: Fill us with your grace.

Third Reading   Invite the Scripture reader to read Mark 14:22–25.

Confirmation   *[Lead the group back to the baptismal font near the Easter candle, where you now drape a red cloth near the white garment.]*

[Invite the group to sing the refrain of "Who Calls You by Name?"]

Teen Prayer Leader 1: Let us pray for those preparing to receive the sacrament of Confirmation, that the Holy Spirit may guide, inspire, and challenge them.

All: Fill us with your grace.

Teen Prayer Leader 2: Let us pray for all who have been confirmed, that they may be filled with the spirit of wisdom, understanding, right judgment, courage, knowledge, reverence, and wonder and awe in God's presence.

All: Fill us with your grace.

Fourth Reading   Invite the Scripture reader to read Acts 2:1–4.

Matrimony   *[Lead the group to a kneeler for two in front of the altar, where you have placed wedding rings and a set of unity candles.]*

[Invite the group to sing the refrain of "Who Calls You by Name?"]

Teen Prayer Leader 1: Let us pray for those who will be married at our parish this year, that they may make Christ the center of their lives and grow in love and devotion to each other.

All: Fill us with your grace.

Teen Prayer Leader 2: Let us pray for those who are married, that they may remain faithful to their wedding vows and bring Christ to life in their marriage.

All: Fill us with your grace.

Fifth Reading   Invite the Scripture reader to read John 2:1–11.

Holy Orders   *[Invite a teen to retrieve the chrism from the baptismal font and place it on or near the ambo, where the Gospel is proclaimed. Lead the group to the ambo, where you have placed a stole.]*

[Invite the group to sing the refrain of "Who Calls You by Name?"]

Teen Prayer Leader 1: Let us pray for all the teens in our parish, that they may be open to sharing their faith in a vocation as a priest, sister, brother, or lay minister.

All: Fill us with your grace.

Teen Prayer Leader 2: Let us pray for priests, that they do not lose heart as they share the Gospel, celebrate the Eucharist, and minister to God's people.

All: Fill us with your grace.

Sixth Reading   Invite the Scripture reader to read Matthew 9:35–38.

Anointing of the Sick   *[Lead the group to a pew in the church, where you have placed the oil of the sick and a pyx.*

[Invite the group to sing the refrain of "Who Calls You by Name?"]

Teen Prayer Leader 1: Let us pray for those who suffer with illness, that God may grant them comfort in body and soul.

All: Fill us with your grace.

Teen Prayer Leader 2: Let us pray for those who have died, especially those whom we hold dear, that they may find peace with Christ.

All: Fill us with your grace.

Seventh Reading   Invite the Scripture reader to read Luke 18:35–43.

17 Jesus Calls Us to Change Our Lives

Themes
- Changing your life
- Living life for God and others
- Spending quiet time with God

Suggested Uses
- As part of a retreat day on the sacrament of Reconciliation
- Prior to the sacrament of Reconciliation
- At the first gathering after Ash Wednesday

Forms of Prayer
- Symbolic prayer
- Music
- Silent prayer
- Reflection
- Journaling
- Scripture

Extra Prayer Ideas
A. Invite the teens to search for and share other stories, fiction and nonfiction, that call us to conversion.
B. Allow the teens to take turns taking home a CD of Christian music. At the start of each class, invite the teen who last had the CD to play part of a song and share his or her own reflection.
C. Ask the teens to reflect on John 14:2, "In my father's house there are many dwelling places . . . I go to prepare a place for you," and how it connects to the song "That's All the Lumber You Sent."
D. During quiet prayer, give the teens a copy of the reflection questions and ask them to write in their journals. Challenge them to make time each day during Lent to write in their journals.

"That's All the Lumber You Sent"

Materials
- ❑ a copy of the CD *Ceili Rain: Say Kay-lee*, by Ceili Rain (Punch Records, 1998)
- ❑ a CD player
- ❑ pieces of wood, one for each teen
- ❑ a red marker or red paint and a paintbrush

Preparation
- Cue the CD to "That's All the Lumber You Sent."
- Collect a piece of wood for each person. On each piece, write in red "Jesus Calls Us to Change Our Lives." Add a red heart. Put the pieces of wood in a box and keep them off to the side of the prayer space.
- Invite an adult leader to prepare a reflection on the theme "The Call to Conversion."

Order of Prayer

Opening Song

Play the song "That's All the Lumber You Sent." Ask the teens to listen carefully to the words. During the refrain only, ask a few teen leaders to come up one at a time and place the pieces of wood in a pile in the center of the space. They should place them in such a way that the writing is hidden from view.

Reflection

Invite the adult leader to come forward and present his or her reflection on the theme "The Call to Conversion." After the reflection, the adult leader poses the following questions for discussion:
- What is the song about?
- How does the song call us to change?
- How is Lent an opportunity for change?

Silent Prayer

Invite the teens to reflect on ways they need to change their lives during Lent. Ask them to spread out in the prayer space or around church so they can give one another physical room to reflect. During silent prayer, ask a few teen leaders to pick up the pieces of wood from the front and give one to each person.

Concluding Song

Play the song "That's All the Lumber You Sent" for a second time. Invite the teens, one at a time, to bring up their pieces of wood while the song is playing. Ask the teen leaders to help the others place the wood in the shape of a cross, with the hearts and the writing facing up.

Before the teens leave, invite each one to take a piece of wood to remember that Jesus calls us to change our lives during Lent.

18

Marian Prayer

Themes
- Saying yes to God and saying no to what is wrong
- Making right choices
- Being open to God's call

Suggested Uses
- As part of a class on Mary
- For a youth-group meeting in the month of May
- As part of a session on making the right choices
- As part of a vocations program

Forms of Prayer
- Music
- Litany
- Traditional prayer
- Reflection
- Art
- Journaling

Extra Prayer Ideas

A. Ask the teens to learn more about one of the devotions to Mary listed in the litany.

B. Invite the teens to pray the living rosary, each teen representing one bead of the rosary. They can hold red candles to represent the Lord's Prayer and blue candles to represent each Hail Mary. After a teen leads a prayer, he or she lights the candle he or she is holding.

C. During the month of May, invite the teens to come before class and pray the rosary each week, using a different set of the mysteries (sorrowful, joyful, glorious, and luminous).

D. Divide the large group into small groups and invite them to create their own litanies to Mary.

E. Offer the teens a selection of holy cards dedicated to Mary or hand out holy cards with the "*Memorare*" printed on the back.

Saying Yes to God

Materials   Gather the following items before beginning the prayer service:
- ❑ a blue candle
- ❑ matches
- ❑ THE CATHOLIC YOUTH BIBLE or another Bible
- ❑ the song "I Say 'Yes,' Lord / Digo 'Sí,' Señor," by Donna Pena
- ❑ six copies of resource 18–A, "Litany of Mary"
- ❑ copies of handout 18–A, "'Memorare,'" one for each teen
- ❑ a statue of Mary

Preparation
- • Ask a teen to prepare the Scripture reading:
  - ◦ Luke 1:26–38 (Mary Says Yes to Being the Mother of God)
- • Ask six teens to prepare the litany on resource 18–A, "Litany of Mary."
- • Place the candle and statue on the prayer table. Light the candle.
- • Teach the song, "I Say 'Yes,' Lord."

Order of Prayer

Call to Prayer   **Prayer Leader:** Mary gave birth to Jesus Christ in order to share him with the world. Mary was completely open to the call of the Spirit. We are inspired by Mary, our mother, to serve God and to serve others. Mary calls us, also, to say yes to God's will in our lives.

Reading   *[Invite the Scripture reader to read Luke 1:26–38.]*

[Direct the group to sing verse one of "I Say 'Yes,' Lord." Allow some quiet time for reflection after they sing.]

Prayer Leader: Reflect on a time when God called you to follow God. Silently thank God for the grace to say yes.

[Pause.]

Prayer Leader: Reflect on a time when you said no to God through your words or actions. Silently ask God's forgiveness for turning away.

[Pause.]

Prayer Leader: Reflect on an area of your life where you have trouble saying yes to God. Silently ask God for the courage to say yes.

[Direct the group to sing verse two of "I Say 'Yes,' Lord." Allow some quiet time for reflection after they sing.]

Litany to Mary

Litany Reader 1: Our response is, "Pray for us."

All: Pray for us.

[Pause for all to respond after each line of the litany.]

Litany Reader 1:

Our Lady of the Snows . . .
Our Lady of Fatima . . .
Our Lady of Lourdes . . .
Our Lady of Nazareth . . .
Our Lady of Guadalupe . . .
Our Lady of Czestochowa . . .

Litany Reader 2:

Madonna of the Rose . . .
Madonna of Miracles . . .
Madonna of the Star . . .
Madonna of the Rosary . . .

Litany Reader 3:

Our Lady, Refuge of Sinners . . .
Our Lady of Sorrows . . .
Our Lady of the Forsaken . . .
Our Lady of Consolation . . .
Our Lady of Help . . .
Our Lady of the Cross . . .

Litany Reader 4:

Mother of Jesus . . .
Mother of Our Church . . .
Mother of the Sick . . .
Mother of the Dying . . .
Mother of Comfort . . .
Mother of Peace . . .

Litany Reader 5:

Our Lady of Grace . . .
Our Lady of Light . . .
Our Lady of Good Counsel . . .
Our Lady of Charity . . .
Our Lady of Wisdom . . .
Our Lady of Every Day . . .
Our Lady of Blessings . . .

Litany Reader 6:

Mary, star of the sea . . .
Mary, mother of us all . . .
Mary, gift of faith . . .
Mary, gift of hope . . .
Mary, gift of love . . .

"Memorare"   *[Distribute a copy of handout 18–A, "Memorare," to each teen.]*

Litany Reader 6: Let us join together in praying the *"Memorare."*

[Direct the group to sing verse one of "I Say 'Yes,' Lord." Allow some quiet time for reflection after they sing.]

Litany of Mary

[Pause for all to respond after each line of the litany.]

Litany Reader 1   Our Lady of the Snows . . .
Our Lady of Fatima . . .
Our Lady of Lourdes . . .
Our Lady of Nazareth . . .
Our Lady of Guadalupe . . .
Our Lady of Czestochowa . . .

Litany Reader 2   Madonna of the Rose . . .
Madonna of Miracles . . .
Madonna of the Star . . .
Madonna of the Rosary . . .

Litany Reader 3   Our Lady, Refuge of Sinners . . .
Our Lady of Sorrows . . .
Our Lady of the Forsaken . . .
Our Lady of Consolation . . .
Our Lady of Help . . .
Our Lady of the Cross . . .

Litany Reader 4   Mother of Jesus . . .
Mother of Our Church . . .
Mother of the Sick . . .
Mother of the Dying . . .
Mother of Comfort . . .
Mother of Peace . . .

Litany Reader 5   Our Lady of Grace . . .
Our Lady of Light . . .
Our Lady of Good Counsel . . .
Our Lady of Charity . . .
Our Lady of Wisdom . . .
Our Lady of Every Day . . .
Our Lady of Blessings . . .

Litany Reader 6   Mary, star of the sea . . .
Mary, mother of us all . . .
Mary, gift of faith . . .
Mary, gift of hope . . .
Mary, gift of love . . .

Let us join together in praying the *"Memorare."*

"Memorare"

Remember, most loving Virgin Mary,
never was it heard
that anyone who turned to you for help,
was left unaided.

Inspired by this confidence,
though burdened by my sins,
I run to your protection
for you are my mother.

Mother of the Word of God,
do not despise my words of pleading
but be merciful and hear my prayer.

Amen.

(This prayer is from *Catholic Household Blessings and Prayers*, by the Bishops' Committee on the Liturgy [Washington, DC: United States Conference of Catholic Bishops (USCCB), 1989], pages 362–363. Copyright © 1989 by the USCCB. All rights reserved.)

19
An Advent Pilgrimage Prayer

Themes
- Journey from Advent to Christmas
- Searching for the Christ child
- Praying with our feet
- Making quiet time for Christ
- What shall we do while we are waiting?

Suggested Uses
- To introduce the Advent season to a youth group or class
- To deflect attention away from the commercial aspects of the season
- As part of an Advent retreat
- At a joint gathering with another parish youth group
- As the centerpiece of an Advent youth-group meeting

Forms of Prayer
- Pilgrimage
- Scripture
- Music
- Symbolic prayer
- Storytelling
- Traditional prayer
- Shared prayer
- Petition
- Silent prayer
- Art

Extra Prayer Ideas
A. Turn this prayer service into a day retreat by adding a discussion, an activity, journal time, or a witness talk to each section.
B. Conduct this prayer service outdoors.
C. After modeling a pilgrimage prayer during the Advent season, challenge the teens to create one for Lent.
D. Supply materials for the teens to make their own Advent wreaths for home prayer with their families.

Are You "He Who Is to Come"?

Materials   Gather the following items before beginning the prayer service:

❑ copies of handout 19–A, "Responses for Advent Pilgrims," one copy for each teen

❑ THE CATHOLIC YOUTH BIBLE or another Bible

❑ the song "Wait for the Lord," by R. Jacques Berthier

❑ a large Advent wreath with candles

❑ matches

❑ the song "Stay Awake," by Christopher Walker

❑ an undecorated Christmas tree

❑ the song "O Christmas Tree" (traditional)

❑ the song "O Come, O Come, Emmanuel" (traditional)

❑ one copy of resource 19–A, "The Great Guest"

Preparation
• Set up the seven stops for the pilgrimage.
• Ask a teen to prepare the Scripture reading:
  ○ Matthew 11:2–11 (Messengers from John the Baptist and Jesus Praises John the Baptist)
• Ask a teen to prepare the story on resource 19–A, "The Great Guest."
• Teach the songs "Wait for the Lord," "Stay Awake," "O Christmas Tree," and "O Come, O Come, Emmanuel."

Order of Prayer

First Stop   *[Lead the group to the reception area of the church or school. Distribute a copy of handout 19–A, "Responses for Advent Pilgrims," to each teen for the prayer responses.]*

Prayer Leader: We ask . . .

All: Are you "he who is to come," or do we look for another?

[Invite the Scripture reader to read Matthew 11:2–11.]

Prayer Leader: How do we recognize Jesus when he comes? In a spirit of welcoming and hospitality. We pray for God's blessings as we continue our journey through Advent to Christmas. Let us always hold a special spirit of hospitality, making friends, family, and even strangers feel welcome. We pray . . .

All: Lord, help us recognize you in everything we see and in everyone we meet. Amen.

[Invite the teens to sing "Wait for the Lord" as they travel to the next stop.]

Second Stop *[Invite the teens to gather around the Advent wreath.]*

> **Prayer Leader:** We ask . . .

All: Are you "he who is to come," or do we look for another?

[Light the appropriate number of candles based on the week of Advent.]

Prayer Leader: How do we recognize Jesus when he comes? In the light of Christ shining through each one of us. We pray for God's blessings as we continue our journey through Advent to Christmas. Let us always keep the light of Christ burning strongly in our hearts and share that light with friends, family, and everyone we meet. We pray . . .

All: Lord, help us to recognize you in everything we see and in everyone we meet. Amen.

[Invite the teens to sing "Stay Awake" as they travel to the next stop.]

Third Stop *[Lead the group to the undecorated Christmas tree, or to a nearby evergreen tree outside.]*

> **Prayer Leader:** We ask . . .

All: Are you "he who is to come," or do we look for another?

[Invite the group to sing "O Christmas Tree."]

Prayer Leader: How do we recognize Jesus when he comes? In God's ever green, everlasting love. We pray for God's blessings as we continue our journey through Advent to Christmas. Let us always remember that God's love is unconditional and everlasting. Help us to share God's love with friends, family, and everyone we meet. We pray . . .

All: Lord, help us recognize you in everything we see and in everyone we meet. Amen.

[Invite the teens to sing "Wait for the Lord" for a second time as they travel to the next stop.]

Fourth Stop *[Lead the group to the parish food pantry or to a display of parish or school outreach efforts.]*

> **Prayer Leader:** We ask . . .

All: Are you "he who is to come," or do we look for another?

[Invite the story reader to read the story on handout 19–A, "The Great Guest."]

Prayer Leader: How do we recognize Jesus when he comes? In the poor, in the hungry, in the homeless, in all in need. We pray for God's blessings as we continue our journey through Advent to Christmas. Let us always reach out to the needy and discover Christ in each of them. Let us challenge our friends, family, and community to do the same. We pray . . .

All: Lord, help us recognize you in everything we see and in everyone we meet. Amen.

[Invite the teens to sing "Stay Awake" for a second time as they travel to the next stop.]

Fifth Stop   *[Lead the group to the twelfth station of the cross, Jesus Dies on the Cross.]*

Prayer Leader: We ask . . .

All: Are you "he who is to come," or do we look for another?

[Invite the teens to offer a prayer for anyone who is sick, suffering, or has died.]

Prayer Leader: How do we recognize Jesus when he comes? In those who are sick and in the families of those who have lost loved ones. We pray for God's blessings as we continue our journey through Advent to Christmas. Let us pray for all those who are sick and suffering, for all those who have died, among our friends, in our families, and in our parish community. We pray . . .

All: Lord, help us recognize you in everything we see and in everyone we meet. Amen.

Sixth Stop   *[Invite the teens to sing "O Come, O Come Emmanuel" as they travel to the next stop.]*

[Lead the teens to a stained-glass window.]

Prayer Leader: We ask . . .

All: Are you "he who is to come," or do we look for another?

[Invite the teens to offer each other a sign of peace.]

Prayer Leader: How do we recognize Jesus when he comes? In all those who work for peace in our world. We pray for God's blessings as we continue our journey through Advent to Christmas. Let us always keep prayers for peace close to our hearts. Let us share the peace of Christ with everyone we meet, and let us call on the Holy Spirit to bring peace to our world this holy season and always. We pray . . .

All: Lord, help us recognize you in everything we see and in everyone we meet. Amen.

[Invite the teens to sing "Wait for the Lord" for a third time as they travel to the last stop.]

Last Stop   *[Lead the teens to the tabernacle where the Blessed Sacrament is reserved, in the chapel or church.]*

Prayer Leader: We ask . . .

All: Are you "he who is to come," or do we look for another?

[Invite the teens to pray silently for a special intention.]

Prayer Leader: How do we recognize Jesus when he comes? In quiet time spent in prayer. We pray for God's blessings as we continue our journey through Advent to Christmas. Let us always find time to talk to God in prayer, in a special way. Let us remember to pray for our friends, family, and parish community this Advent season and always. We pray . . .

All: Lord, help us recognize you in everything we see and in everyone we meet.

Prayer Leader: May God keep you and your family safe and well this holiday season. In the name of the Father, and of the Son, and of the Holy Spirit.

All: Amen.

Responses for Advent Pilgrims

[Use at each stop.]

Prayer Leader   We ask . . .

All   Are you "he who is to come," or do we look for another?

Prayer Leader   We pray . . .

All   Lord, help us to recognize you in everything we see and in everyone we meet. Amen.

The Great Guest

It happened one day at the year's white end—
Two neighbors called on their old-time friend;
And they found the shop so meager and mean,
Made merry with a hundred boughs of green.
Conrad, the cobbler, was stitching, a face ashine,
But stopped as he twitched a twine;
"Old friends, good news! At dawn today,
As the roosters were scaring the night away,
The Lord appeared in a dream to me,
And said, 'I am coming your Guest to be!'
So I have been busy with feet astir
Strewing the floor with branches of fir.
The wall is washed and the shelf is shined,
And over the rafter the holly twined.
He comes today, and the table is spread
With milk and honey and wheaten bread."

His friends went home; and his face grew still
As he watched for the shadow across the sill.
He lived all the moments over and over,
When the Lord should enter the lowly door—
The knock, the call, the latch pulled up,
The lighted face, the offered cup.
He would wash the feet where the spikes had been,
He would kiss the hands where the nails went in,
And then at last he would sit with Him
And break the bread as the day grew dim.

While the cobbler mused, there passed his pane
A beggar drenched by the driving rain.
He called him in front from the stony street.
And gave him shoes for his bruised feet.
The beggar went and there came a crone,
Her face with wrinkles of sorrow sewn.
A bundle of coal bowed her back,
And she was spent with the wrench and rack.
He gave her his loaf and steadied her load
As she took her way on the weary road.
Then to his door came a little child,
Lost and afraid in a world so wild,
In the big, dark world. Catching her up
He gave her milk in the waiting cup.
And led her home to her mother's arms,
Out of the reach of the world's alarms.

The day went down in the crimson west,
And with it the hope of the blessed Guest,
And Conrad sighed as the world turned gray:
"Why is it, Lord, that your feet delay?
Did you forget that this is the day?"
Then soft in the silence a voice he heard:
"Lift up your heart, for I kept my word.
Three times I came to your friendly door;
Three times my shadow was on your floor.
I was the beggar with bruised feet;
I was the old woman you gave food to eat;
I was the child on the nameless street."

(*Sower's Seeds Aplenty: 100 Stories of Wit, Whimsy, and Wisdom for Life's Travels*, edited by Brian Cavanaugh [Mahwah, NJ: Paulist Press, 1996], pages 30–32. Copyright © 1996 by Brian Cavanaugh. Used with permission.)

20 $\mathcal{A}$ Lenten Prayer Service

Themes
- Respect for the cross
- The sacrifice of the cross
- What the cross means to us
- Carrying the cross
- Take your troubles to the cross
- Good Friday faith

Suggested Uses
- At the start of Lent
- Right before Holy Week
- During a Lenten retreat or a retreat exploring the sacrifice of Jesus

Forms of Prayer
- Music
- Reflection
- Petition
- Poetry
- Symbolic prayer
- Liturgical Prayer
- Art

Extra Prayer Ideas

A. Invite the rest of the parish or school community to drive nails into the large cross, either on Ash Wednesday or during Lent.

B. Invite the teens to create their own pendants using nails, wire, and a cord.

C. Start a discussion about the ways our society misuses or devalues the symbol of the cross.

D. Pray one part of "Hang It on the Cross" (resource 20–B) each week of Lent.

E. If the teens in your parish do not have a cross or crucifix at home, help them make one.

F. Make pretzels and share this prayer during Lent:

> Heavenly Father,
> Please bless these little breads we call pretzels.
> May they be a reminder to us of the special season of Lent.
> May the little arms remind us that we are children of God.
> May the big arms remind us that you protect us with your loving arms.
> May the three holes remind us of the mystery of your Trinity.
> In the name of the Father, and of the Son, and of the Holy Spirit.
> Amen.

G. Create Holy Thursday invitations for the teens. One side of the card should say, "Jesus of Nazareth requests the honor of your presence at a banquet to be given in his honor," and the other side should say, "Please join us for the Holy Thursday celebration of the Last Supper and the First Eucharist, the start of the solemn memorial of the Triduum." You can also add the time that the liturgy will take place.

At a Crossroads

Materials

Gather the following items before beginning the prayer service:
- ❏ a copy of the CD *Change Your World*, by Michael W. Smith (Reunion Records, 1993)
- ❏ a CD player
- ❏ prayer journals or paper, one for each participant
- ❏ pens or pencils, one for each participant
- ❏ copies of handout 20–A, "Prayer Journal Questions," one for each teen
- ❏ two copies of resource 20–A, "Prayers of Petition for Lent"
- ❏ one copy of resource 20–B, "'Hang It on the Cross'"
- ❏ a large wooden cross
- ❏ a basket of nails, one nail for each teen
- ❏ a basket of hammers (five or six)

Preparation

- Build a large wooden cross of soft wood, such as pine.
- Place the cross in the center of your prayer space, with a small basket of nails and a basket of hammers nearby.
- Ask two teens to prepare the petitions on resource 20–A, "Prayers of Petition for Lent."
- Ask another teen to prepare the poem on resource 20–B, "'Hang It on the Cross.'"
- Cue the CD to the song "Cross of Gold."

Order of Prayer

Call to Prayer

Prayer Leader: We are an Easter people. We would rather forget Good Friday. We like a warm and fuzzy faith. There is no place for metal nails piercing flesh, for pain, suffering, and death. Good Friday puts us face to face with the stark reality of the cross, of Jesus suffering and broken, and of our brokenness in body and spirit.

Good Friday demands that we ask:
- What does the cross mean to us?
- Why is there a cross in our worship space?
- Why is there a cross on the outside of our building?
- Why are there crosses on the walls of our rooms?
- Why do we wear a cross of gold?

[Play the song "Cross of Gold."]

Prayer Journal

Distribute copies of handout 20–A, "Prayer Journal Questions," prayer journals or paper, and pens or pencils to the teens. Ask them to spread out and journal on the questions quietly. When all appear to be finished writing, gather the group around the cross and continue with prayer.

Prayers of Petition

Reader 1: Our response is, "Lord, give us courage to carry your cross." **All respond.**

Reader 1: We pray for the courage to face our own personal Good Fridays. **All respond.**

Reader 2: We pray for the courage to take a stand, to stand up for what we believe. **All respond.**

Reader 1: We pray that the message of the cross will pierce our hearts. **All respond.**

Reader 2: We pray that our faith will become a passion, a fire of love living within. **All respond.**

Reader 1: We pray for the ability to set aside secular icons and focus on the mystery and majesty of the cross. **All respond.**

Reader 2: We pray that through us, others may experience the hope and promise of the cross. **All respond.**

Reader 1: We pray for the courage to struggle through our Good Fridays so we may truly celebrate Easter. **All respond.**

"Hang It on the Cross"

Poem Reader:

If you have a secret sorrow,
A burden or a loss,
An aching for healing . . .
Hang It On the Cross.

If worry steals your sleep
And makes you turn and toss,
If your heart is feeling heavy . . .
Hang It On the Cross.

Every obstacle to faith
Or doubt you come across,
Every prayer unanswered . . .
Hang It On the Cross.

For Christ has borne
Our brokenness
And dearly paid the cost
To turn our trials to triumph . . .
Hanging On the Cross.

(*Hang It On the Cross* prayer card, by Lisa O. Engelhardt)

Walk of Nails

Invite the teens each to come forward and hammer a nail into the cross.

Prayer Journal Questions

Good Friday demands that we ask the following questions:

- What does the cross mean to us?
- Why is there a cross in our worship space?
- Why is there a cross on the outside of our building?
- Why are there crosses on the walls of our rooms?
- Why do we wear a cross of gold?

Prayers of Petition for Lent

Reader 1   Our response is "Lord, give us courage to carry your cross."
All respond.

Reader 1   We pray for the courage to face our own personal Good Fridays.
All respond.

Reader 2   We pray for the courage to take a stand, to stand up for what we believe.
All respond.

Reader 1   We pray that the message of the cross will pierce our hearts.
All respond.

Reader 2   We pray that our faith will become a passion, a fire of love living within.
All respond.

Reader 1   We pray for the ability to set aside secular icons and focus on the mystery and majesty of the cross.
All respond.

Reader 2   We pray that through us, others may experience the hope and promise of the cross.
All respond.

Reader 1   We pray for the courage to struggle through our Good Fridays so we may truly celebrate Easter.
All respond.

"Hang It On the Cross"

If you have a secret sorrow,
A burden or a loss,
An aching for healing . . .
Hang It On the Cross.

If worry steals your sleep
And makes you turn and toss,
If your heart is feeling heavy . . .
Hang It On the Cross.

Every obstacle to faith
Or doubt you come across,
Every prayer unanswered . . .
Hang It On the Cross.

For Christ has borne
Our brokenness
And dearly paid the cost
To turn our trials to triumph . . .
Hanging On the Cross.

(*Hang It On the Cross* prayer card, by Lisa O. Engelhardt. Copyright © 2001 by Abbey Press, St. Meinrad, IN. Used with permission.)

21

*J*esus, Come Heal Us

Themes
- Turning to Jesus for help
- Jesus has the power to heal us
- Letting prayer give us strength
- We all deal with demons
- Supporting one another in prayer

Suggested Uses
- At a class or meeting on the miracles of Jesus
- To help teens understand that God is there for them in their struggles
- To empower teens to name their demons or struggles

Forms of Prayer
- Scripture
- Symbolic prayer
- Shared prayer
- Petition
- Traditional prayer
- Storytelling

Extra Prayer Ideas
A. Invite an older teen or young adult to give a witness talk covering the following points:
   - It is okay to have doubts.
   - Turn your doubts over to God.
   - When we ask God for help, God will provide.
B. Divide the large group into small groups of four or five. Assign each small group one of the following miracles to read and reflect on:
   - Matthew 20:29–34 (Jesus Heals Two Blind Men)
   - Mark 1:40–45 (Jesus Cleanses a Leper)
   - Mark 5:21–34 (Jesus Heals a Woman)
   - Luke 5:17–26 (Jesus Heals a Paralytic)
   - Luke 7:1–10 (Jesus Heals a Centurion's Servant)
   - Luke 17:11–19 (Jesus Cleanses Ten Lepers)

   Invite the small groups to share their responses with the larger group.
C. Read John 20:19–31. Ask one teen to take the role of Thomas and eleven others to take the roles of the other Apostles and act out the passage in three acts. For the first act, depict Thomas with the Apostles after they've seen Jesus when Thomas was absent. What does Thomas say? How do the others try to convince him that Jesus is alive? For the second act, recreate the scene when Thomas meets Jesus. For the third act, have Thomas meet some friends and describe his experience.

Casting Out the Demons

Materials
Gather the following items before beginning the prayer service:
- ❑ votive candles, one for each separate prayer space
- ❑ candle holders, one for each votive candle
- ❑ matches
- ❑ four copies of resource 21–A, "Scripture Reading: Mark 9:14–29"
- ❑ a pillar candle

Preparation
- This prayer service is designed for six to seven people. If you have a larger group, create small groups of six to seven and be sure each group has its own private space for prayer. Assign a leader for each group, and explain the leader's role.
- Ask four people in each small group to prepare the Scripture reading on resource 21–A, "Scripture Reading: Mark 9:14–29."
- Prior to the prayer service, you may choose to brainstorm a general list of demons, or evils, in society.
- Light a votive candle in the center of each prayer space.

Order of Prayer

Sign of the Cross
Begin the prayer service by praying the sign of the cross.

Reading
[Direct the four Scripture readers to read Mark 9:14–29, as outlined in the following script.]

Reader 1: When they came to the disciples, they saw a great crowd around them and some scribes arguing with them. When the whole crowd saw him, they were immediately overcome with awe, and they ran forward to greet him.

Reader 2: He asked them, "What are you arguing about with them?"

Reader 3: Someone from the crowd answered him, "Teacher, I brought you my son; he has a spirit that makes him unable to speak; and whenever it seizes him, it dashes him down; and he foams and grinds his teeth and becomes rigid; and I asked your disciples to cast him out, but they could not do so."

Reader 2: He answered them: "You faithless generation, how much longer must I be among you? How much longer must I put up with you? Bring him to me."

Reader 1: And they brought the boy to him. When the spirit saw him, immediately it convulsed the boy, and he fell on the ground and rolled about, foaming at the mouth.

Reader 2: Jesus asked the father, "How long has this been happening to him?"

Reader 3: And he said, "From childhood. It has often cast him into the fire and into the water, to destroy him; but if you are able to do anything, have pity on us and help us."

Reader 2: "If you are able!—All things can be done for the one who believes."

Reader 3: Immediately the father of the child cried out, "I believe; help my unbelief!"

Reader 1: When Jesus saw that a crowd came running, he rebuked the unclean spirit, saying to it:

Reader 2: "You spirit who keeps this boy from speaking and hearing, I command you, come out of him, and never enter him again!"

Reader 1: After crying out and convulsing him terribly, it came out, and the boy was like a corpse, so that most of them said, "He is dead." But Jesus took him by the hand and lifted him up, and he was able to stand.

Reader 4: When he had entered the house, his disciples asked him privately, "Why could we not cast it out?"

Reader 2: He said to them, "This kind can come out only through prayer."

Shared Prayers to Cast Out Demons

If you brainstormed a general list of demons in society, you may use that list during this section of the prayer.

Pass the lighted pillar candle slowly around the group. Ask that each teen complete the following prayer before passing the candle on to the next person:

Lord, please cast out the demon of . . .

Shared Prayers for Faith

Pass the candle around the group again. This time, ask that each teen pray the following prayer before passing the candle on to the next person:

Lord, help my unbelief.

The Lord's Prayer

Invite the teens to join hands and softly pray the Lord's Prayer together. When they are done praying, direct them to leave the worship space quietly.

Scripture Reading: Mark 9:14–29

Reader 1   When they came to the disciples, they saw a great crowd around them and some scribes arguing with them. When the whole crowd saw him, they were immediately overcome with awe, and they ran forward to greet him.

Reader 2   He asked them, "What are you arguing about with them?"

Reader 3   Someone from the crowd answered him, "Teacher, I brought you my son; he has a spirit that makes him unable to speak; and whenever it seizes him, it dashes him down; and he foams and grinds his teeth and becomes rigid; and I asked your disciples to cast him out, but they could not do so."

Reader 2   He answered them: "You faithless generation, how much longer must I be among you? How much longer must I put up with you? Bring him to me."

Reader 1   And they brought the boy to him. When the spirit saw him, immediately it convulsed the boy, and he fell on the ground and rolled about, foaming at the mouth.

Reader 2   Jesus asked the father, "How long has this been happening to him?"

Reader 3   And he said, "From childhood. It has often cast him into the fire and into the water, to destroy him; but if you are able to do anything, have pity on us and help us."

Reader 2   "If you are able!—All things can be done for the one who believes."

Reader 3   Immediately the father of the child cried out, "I believe; help my unbelief!"

Reader 1   When Jesus saw that a crowd came running, he rebuked the unclean spirit, saying to it:

Reader 2   "You spirit who keeps this boy from speaking and hearing, I command you, come out of him, and never enter him again!"

Reader 1   After crying out and convulsing him terribly, it came out, and the boy was like a corpse, so that most of them said, "He is dead." But Jesus took him by the hand and lifted him up, and he was able to stand.

Reader 4   When he had entered the house, his disciples asked him privately, "Why could we not cast it out?"

Reader 2   He said to them, "This kind can come out only through prayer."

22

Jesus, the Light of the World

Themes
- Reflecting the light of Christ
- Letting your light shine

Suggested Uses
- To help the teens recognize and share the light of Christ
- As an affirmation prayer
- As a prayer after a difficult national or world event
- As an evening prayer on a retreat weekend
- As an early part of a Confirmation preparation program
- To encourage teens who are experiencing tough times

Forms of Prayer
- Symbolic prayer
- Scripture
- Litany
- Silent prayer
- Petition
- Mantra
- Affirmation
- Shared prayer

Extra Prayer Ideas
A. Invite the teens to write out the following mantra prayer and tape it to a mirror in their home so they can say it every time they look in the mirror:
    You are the light of the world!
    I am the light of the world!

B. Collect various light sources, such as candles, flashlights, lamps, camping lanterns, cutouts of lightning bolts, a picture of a streetlamp, and so on. Invite the teens to choose one and to describe how they are similar to that light source.

C. Encourage the teens to write daily in their journal, starting with the following entries:
    Jesus lights my way by . . .
    I can reflect the light of Christ by . . .
    I can let the light of Christ shine through me by . . .

D. Divide the large group into small groups of six to seven teens. Provide a full-length mirror for each small group. Invite them to write on the mirrors, with soap or other washable writing material, ways to reflect the light. Then invite them to walk around the prayer space and read what the other groups shared.

A Lighthouse Prayer

Materials

Gather the following items before beginning the prayer service:

❑ a lighthouse statue
❑ a large blue or seashore-print cloth
❑ several boxes of various sizes
❑ several hand mirrors
❑ several votive candles
❑ several taper candles
❑ small candles, one for each participant
❑ matches
❑ THE CATHOLIC YOUTH BIBLE or another Bible
❑ two copies of resource 22–A, "Litany of Light and Thanksgiving"
❑ copies of handout 22–A, "Mirror," one for each participant
❑ one copy of resource 22–B, "Prayer of Petition for Those in Darkness"
❑ the song "Blessed Are They," by David Haas

Preparation

- Set up several boxes of varying heights and cover them with the blue seashore or print cloth. Place the lighthouse statue at the top and the hand mirrors on each level. Place one votive candle on each level, and place a few tapers nearby.
- Ask one teen to prepare the Scripture reading:
  ○ John 1:1–5 (The Light Shines in the Darkness)
- Ask two teens to prepare the litany on resource 22–A, "Litany of Light and Thanksgiving"
- Ask one teen to prepare the prayer on resource 22–B, "Prayer of Petition for Those in Darkness"
- Teach the song "Blessed Are They."

Order of Prayer

Jesus Lights the Way

Prayer Leader:

Lord, in many ways, you are like a lighthouse on our life's journey.
You are a beacon of hope for the weary and the lost.
You guide us to the right path when we lose our way.
And we can always set our course by following you.

You are the Light of the World.
We are the Light of the World.

Amen.

Reading   Invite the Scripture reader to read John 1:1–5.

Litany of Light and Thanksgiving   *[Explain to the group that everyone will give the response after each line of the litany is read. Be sure the litany readers know to pause after they read each line.]*

Reader 1: Our response is, "Thank you for your light."

All: Thank you for your light.

Reader 1: You shone in the first light of Christmas.
    All respond.

Reader 2: You brought the light of love to the world.
    All respond.

Reader 1: You taught us to see the light in ourselves.
    All respond.

Reader 2: You died so darkness would never win again.
    All respond.

Reader 1: You rose on Easter in the light of glory.
    All respond.

Reader 2: You guide us on our way to the Father.
    All respond.

Reader 1: You are hope for all who are weary.
    All respond.

Reader 2: You set a course for us to follow.
    All respond.

Reader 1: You are the way, the truth, and the light.
    All respond.

We Reflect the Light of Christ   **Prayer Leader:**
    Lord, lighthouses in the early days used mirrors to reflect and increase the reach of their light so they could be seen for miles.
    You call us to reflect your light in our lives.
    You challenge us to magnify your light for others.
    Help us to look in our own mirrors and discover your light within.

    You are the light of the world.
    We are the light of the world.

    Amen.

[Invite the teens to quietly reflect on an area of their lives where they have failed to reflect the light of Christ.]

[Distribute handout 22–A, "Mirror," to the teens. Invite them to think of a way they can reflect the light of Christ. After a few minutes, invite them to write a few words regarding the way they can reflect the light of Christ.]

Let the Light of Christ Shine Through You

Prayer Leader:

Lord, help us to be lighthouses for others on their life's journey.
Allow your light to shine brightly through us.
Help us to share your light with all we meet, especially those in need.
Keep us safe from the darkness that hates your light.

You are the light of the world.
We are the light of the world.

Amen.

Prayers of Petition

[Explain to the group that everyone will give the response after each line of the petition is read. Be sure the petition reader knows to pause after reading each line.]

Petition Reader: Our response is, "Help us share your light."

All: Help us share your light.

Petition Reader:

We pray for all those searching for meaning in their lives . . .
We pray for all those grieving after the loss of a loved one . . .
We pray for the brokenhearted . . .
We pray for all those who feel lost or weary . . .
We pray for all those gathered today . . .

Concluding Song and Candle Procession

Invite the teens to sing "Blessed Are They." While singing, they come forth, one at a time, to light a small candle that symbolizes their prayer.

Litany of Light and Thanksgiving

[Pause for response after reading each line of the litany.]

Reader 1   Our response is, "Thank you for your light."

All   Thank you for your light.

Reader 1   You shone in the first light of Christmas.
         All respond.

Reader 2   You brought the light of love to the world.
         All respond.

Reader 1   You taught us to see the light in ourselves.
         All respond.

Reader 2   You died so darkness would never win again.
         All respond.

Reader 1   You rose on Easter in the light of glory.
         All respond.

Reader 2   You guide us on our way to the Father.
         All respond.

Reader 1   You are hope for all who are weary.
         All respond.

Reader 2   You set a course for us to follow.
         All respond.

Reader 1   You are the way, the truth, and the light.
         All respond.

Mirror

Handout 22–A: Permission to reproduce is granted. © 2006 by Saint Mary's Press.

Prayer of Petition for Those in Darkness

[Pause for response after reading each line of the petition]

Reader Our response is, "Help us share your light."

All Help us share your light.

Reader We pray for all those searching for meaning in their lives . . .
We pray for all those grieving after the loss of a loved one . . .
We pray for the brokenhearted . . .
We pray for all those who feel lost or weary . . .
We pray for all those gathered today . . .

Index of Prayer Forms

Music

Petition

Pilgrimage

Poetry

Reflection

Sacramental Prayer

Scripture

Shared Prayer

Silent Prayer

Storytelling

Symbolic Prayer

Traditional Prayer

Acknowledgments

The scriptural quotations contained herein are from the New Revised Standard Version of the Bible, Catholic Edition. Copyright © 1993 and 1989 by the Division of Christian Education of the National Council of the Churches of Christ in the United States of America. All rights reserved.

The excerpt on the dedication page is the refrain of the song "Farewell Blessing," by James Hansen. Copyright © 1991 by Gary Hardin and James Hansen. Published by OCP Publications, 5536 NE Hassalo, Portland, OR 97213. All rights reserved. Used with permission.

The excerpt on page 13 is by Albert Camus and found at "Quote DB," at *www.quotedb.com/quotes/1977*, accessed December 13, 2005.

Resource 11–B, "'The Parable of the Talents,'" is adapted from *Growing with Jesus: Sixteen Half-day, Full-day, and Overnight Retreats That Help Children Celebrate and Share the Light of Christ,* by Maryann Hakowski (Notre Dame, IN: Ave Maria Press, 1993), pages 238–239. Copyright © 1993 by Ave Maria Press, Notre Dame, IN 46556. Used with permission.

The story "A Bundle of Sticks" by Bill Gordh on resource 12–A is adapted from "'A Bundle of Sticks,'" on page 64 is by Bill Gordh and taken from *Sesame Street Parents Magazine,* December 1998/January 1999 issue.

The story "The Inner Lion" on resource 14–A is adapted from *Existential Metapsychiatry,* by Thomas Hora (New York: Seabury Press, 1977), pages 20–21. Copyright © 1977 by Seabury Press.

The prayer on handout 18–A is from *Catholic Household Blessings and Prayers,* by the Bishops' Committee on the Liturgy (Washington, DC: United States Conference of Catholic Bishops [USCCB], 1989), pages 362–363. Copyright © 1989 by the USCCB. All rights reserved.

The story on resource 19–A is from *Sower's Seeds Aplenty: 100 Stories of Wit, Whimsy, and Wisdom for Life's Travels,* edited by Brian Cavanaugh (Mahwah, NJ: Paulist Press, 1996), pages 30–32. Copyright © 1996 by Brian Cavanaugh. Used with permission.

The poem on resource 20–B, "'Hang It On the Cross,'" is from the *Hang It On the Cross* prayer card, by Lisa O. Engelhardt. Copyright © 2001 by Abbey Press, St. Meinrad, IN. Used with permission.

To view copyright terms and conditions for Internet materials cited here, log on to the home pages for the referenced Web sites.

During this book's preparation, all citations, facts, figures, names, addresses, telephone numbers, Internet URLs, and other pieces of information cited within were verified for accuracy. The authors and Saint Mary's Press staff have made every attempt to reference current and valid sources, but we cannot guarantee the content of any source, and we are not responsible for any changes that may have occurred since our verification. If you find an error in, or have a question or concern about, any of the information or sources listed within, please contact Saint Mary's Press.